MAKE YOUR OWN CHANGE

MAKE YOUR OWN CHANGE

By Nancy Means Wright

Illustrations by Lachlan Field

Down East Books / Camden, Maine

Contents

Other books by Nancy Means Wright:

The Losing
Down the Strings

For Spencer

Acknowledgments

The author wishes to thank all those friends, neighbors, and relatives, and offspring of same, who allowed me to describe (with loving if roguish intent) the antics of themselves and others, living and deceased; and who helped on occasion to jog my memory. A few names and dates are changed; most are not. To my own family I can only say: "Sorry again, gang. But you'll live it down."

THE HOUSE

*Change is not made without inconvenience,
even from worse to better.*

Richard Hooker, 16th century

No Room at the Inn:
or, Plumb Out of Patience

ONE SPRING MORNING between classes at Proctor Academy, the boys' school in Andover, New Hampshire, where my husband and I both taught, I began a novel. It was about a faculty wife, a latter-day Madame Bovary, trapped in a labyrinth of locker rooms full of men and boys. I locked myself into the bedroom to write it while Gary and Lesley, our two young children, bled outside in the hall. "I can't love you any more — I can't!" my heroine wept as her redhaired husband jogged off in his green sweatpants.

At that time we were spending three months of the year with Spencer's parents in Vermont, and the other nine in a tiny apartment in a boys' dormitory. I tutored remedial reading and put on plays, while Spence taught history and coached hockey or football as the season allowed. Evenings the apartment trembled as his quarterbacks leaped over his mother's horsehair sofa to smash into the rug for a first down.

I was just completing chapter one when we were transferred into the biggest dorm on campus, nicknamed The Zoo. Our living room was divided from the rest of the apartment by a staircase where thirty-five boys swept up and down at frantic intervals. A thin wall separated our kitchen from the boys' Butt Room. In the bath and bedrooms the ancient pipes offered a direct line of communication between ourselves and the upstairs. I was sitting on the toilet one night when a disembodied voice hissed down: "Oh, Mrs. Wright — I see you-hoo-oo."

"I want modern plumbing or I'm leaving!" I shrieked at my husband (while a dozen grinning ears clung to the far side of the wall).

But where to go? I'd run out of parents years ago. My older sister, Grace, was struggling with an adolescent child in a mini-apartment. One brother was abroad, working for the State Department; the other occupied a single room in Florida, where he pounded out pop tunes for a living on a rented piano. There was no room in anyone's inn for a runaway wife and two brawling children.

When Grace took a cottage at Cape Cod that June the children and I went with her, leaving Spence to make the summer pilgrimage to the in-laws' alone. We all waved good-bye as he drove off in the old green Chrysler, his ruddy face set like a sail toward the West, his lower lip sucking in and out the way it did when he had something on his mind — a play-off game, or a way to keep his marriage together.

In his pocket was our life savings: $250 in cash. He received $3500 a year at school (plus "room" and board) — a salary low even for the late fifties — with a quarter of that going toward the M.A. he'd been earning summers at the university. I had just been promoted to Reading Department Head for $800. The car was of dubious vintage: he'd bought it the fall he met me on the ship after a summer of cycling in Europe. I had fifty cents in my pocket then and five hundred colored postcards of ruined abbeys and leaning towers. Six weeks later he married me, he said, because my maiden name was Means. I married him, I replied, because he had red hair, and as I was nearsighted, I could always find him in a crowd. We were poor in those days, but happy.

While the children and I built sand castles at the Cape, Spence searched for a place of our own on Vermont soil. It had to be Vermont. Eight generations of Wrights, descended from Abel Wright, born in Connecticut in 1631, were buried in Addison County cemeteries: he wanted to connect roots. He didn't tell me at the time that Abel's wife had been been scalped, while Abel lived to be a robust ninety-two. He maneuvered the old Chrysler up rocky hills and down rutted roads. He knocked on doors and tracked farmers into the bowels of their barns to ask if they had land to part with. Perhaps it was the monomania in his blue eyes or the mop of coppery curls, but he came up with offers on every hand. He narrowed the search to three towns: Weybridge (his father's birthplace), Whiting, and Cornwall. The last was his preference, a town of some eight hundred souls, of apple orchards and dairy farms. And finally, to eight properties, all of them $4000 and up. The most we could manage at that time, even with borrowing, was $2500.

One morning Ben Field, an octogenarian farmer who had an egg route, stopped by the Wright Sr. manse, where Spence was mending his parents' fence, and said: "You damn fool. You're running up and down the countryside when the place you want's right under your nose!" And he pointed "downstreet."

"You don't mean the old blacksmith place?" said Spence, leaning into the fence, biting down on his corncob pipe.

"The same," replied Ben.

"But that hasn't been lived in for twenty years. The house is in a state of collapse! Anyway, I heard by the grapevine, they wouldn't sell."

The owner was a titian-haired former schoolteacher named Vivian LeDuc who lived beside what was once the Cornwall General Store and Post Office — the place still held its counters, coffee grinder, and post boxes. It was enough for her to keep up; she wanted to sell the blacksmith property. But her estranged husband, who lived somewhere downcountry, had doubts.

"Ever ask?" said Ben, who, being an eggman, a former selectman, and chairman of the hospital board, had his finger on the pulse of things in town.

That afternoon Spence drove up to Vivian's house in the big green Chrysler New Yorker. It was his first mistake. "The place might be for sale for $3600," Vivian said, her eyes reflecting the shine he'd just put on the car.

"But the house is crumbling into its foundation," Spence argued, "one more big wind and —"

"Thirty-six hundred," Vivian said, her green eyes squinted to meet his.

Spencer drove slowly back up Route 30 to the "Brown House," as it was familiarly called. From the road it was barely visible where it crouched behind a jungle of wild grass and burdock. He parked in the driveway and sat awhile — his cheeks pink with sun, his eyes glazed over. The tangle of weeds became a smooth green lawn, the house a handsome "Colonial." Beyond, a dozen maple and locust trees stretched tall against the soft swell of Bread Loaf Mountain. The locusts showered fragrant June blossoms on the roof like rice on a bride.

An ancient and used bride, of course. Frank Brown, who lived there back in the late nineteenth century, was a blacksmith who came to work as a day laborer for the owner of the stone smithy across the street. Alert and dexterous, Brown became a prosperous smith, and was able to purchase the house, along with its barn and horse stalls. A widower by then, he raised his daughters May and Jenny, and a yard full of lilac, red chokeberry, and bridal wreath. The ménage-à-trois was so close-knit that when Homer Cobb, the town treasurer, who lived in the old Medical College, wanted to marry May Brown, he got two for the price of one. Refusing to part, the sisters moved hand-in-hand after Frank's death into the Cobb House. They stuck together to the end, Jenny succumbing within hours of May, their demise observed by a double funeral. The Cobb house later became the Stanley Wright house, acquired one day at auction, complete with fourteen rooms, outhouses, and crematorium, when my mother-in-law got carried away by the bidding. Jenny's diaries, detailing the nineteenth-century weather, and cancelled checks from the Cornwall treasury, changed hands with it. The Brown and Cobb houses had long been connected in local legend. Now, it seemed, chance might again unite the two.

Spence called me up at the Cape to describe the possible union. Over the wire his voice crackled with emotion. My heart leaped as I envisioned this white manse against a periwinkle sky, more wonderful than any of the colored postcards I had brought home from Europe.

"With an apple orchard across the street?" I said.

"In bloom, every spring. Of course it will take a little work."

"Sure, sure," I said. "And a rosebush by the kitchen door. Pink or yellow, did you say?"

"Yellow," he said. "And $3600. She wouldn't come down."

"Buy it, buy it," I urged. And closed my eyes to imagine the tumble of yellow petals against the turquoise mountains, the children and I barefoot among them.

We went back to Vivian LeDuc — on foot. Two visits later they settled on a price of $3000; $250 down, $500 in a promissory note, $1000 in a demand note, and the rest forthcoming through a bank loan. He drove to the Cape to pick us up. It was a joyous ride back to Vermont. I pelted him with questions, while the children crooned in their padded seats. He tried to explain why we couldn't move in at once.

"A little restoration," he said, knocking his pipe against the car door. He flung out vague nouns like roof, chimney, walls, ceiling.

"Built in 1796, you said? Ah, ghosts of Christmas Past . . . ."

The first decade of my life had been lived in almost as many houses. When my father died, my mother removed the two of us into a girls' boarding school — where I spent five long years under the sharp nose of its Presbyterian headmistress. And then there was a women's college, and the all-boys school. At last, I exulted, I was going home!

"Of course we might want to stay with the folks again for the winter holidays while I'm getting it fixed up," he said.

"You think so?" I sucked in my lip.

Of the fourteen rooms in "the folks' " house, only two were livable in winter. We spent Thanksgiving and Christmas huddled around the kerosene stove: Spence and I and the children, his parents, his younger brother Dan, and a diminutive Yankee grandmother whose self-appointed job was to split wood for the kitchen woodstove. Through it all the senior Wrights tried to maintain a measure of dignity. After all, Stan Wright was Director of Admissions at nearby Middlebury College; the president and his wife were frequent visitors to the house. The family pride slipped rapidly the evening Stan went sailing across the kitchen floor on a frozen diaper, with a roar that was heard around the county.

The final crisis, though, came on Christmas morning when

my mother-in-law, Ruth, who had fought for years to observe the ceremonies of Christmas in the face of the spartan Wrights, stepped downstairs, aglow in a pink wrapper, to find The Tree, dragged home the night before from the Green Mountain National Forest, stripped of its lower ornaments; and below, a third of the presents vandalized. Three-year-old Gary had crept down before dawn and quietly assailed the wrappings. I could only imagine his eyes, as round and bright as the colored balls that hung above the mountain of gifts. When I arrived on the scene he was removing a lacy slip, size 18, from its waxy box: "I love it," said my mother-in-law, a quiver on her lips as she folded it back into the shredded tissue.

"Or we could stay at the lake again," Spence suggested.

"Unh uh," I said. "Lesley's too big now for the bureau drawer."

Back in the twenties, Ruth's father, Charles Ashworth, had built a summer place on Lake Dunmore, a gem of a lake at the foot of Mount Mooslamoo, once frequented by the Green Mountain Boys. The "camp," where we spent two weeks each June packed in with the other in-and-out-laws, was a living illustration of Norman Rockwell's famous sketch that shows the husband grinning good-bye to a station wagon full of guests heading north, while his wife stares with dismay at a carload pulling in from the south.

Behind the big camp was a smaller one, built by Spence and his father to serve as a hunting lodge. The place was to be planted with poison ivy and broken glass, according to Stan Wright, to repel intruders, but luckily for us at the time, he hadn't gotten around to it. We went in, the Christmas after Gary stole the show, with kids, supplies, and toys on our backs. There was a bed for ourselves and Gary; Lesley was assigned to a bureau drawer. We melted snow to warm her bottle, rinsed the rancid diapers in outdoor drifts, gazed through the picture window at the icy lake, and congratulated ourselves that we were at last alone. But when we tried to smile, our faces cracked with the cold. The kerosene heater gave as much heat as a cigarette in a barn. Lesley's voice was a frozen chirp from the drawer. It was too cold even to make love; we couldn't bear to take off our clothes.

The memory of the lake in winter numbed our thoughts, and we settled down to the long drive back to Vermont. "We're here,"

Spence announced four hours later, skidding to a stop in Cornwall. He flung out an arm to sweep in a grassy vista that resembled a Kansas wheat field.

I squinted. Through the weeds I made out a low-slung, weatherbeaten house that looked as if it had been picked up by Dorothy's cyclone and dropped on its rear end in Vermont. The house sloped downhill to culminate in a back stoop like the footbone disconnected from the ankle bone. In the side yard, near a yellow rosebush that had fallen to thorn, was a rusted pump, full of salamanders — "Blinded," I was told, "from generations of darkness. But don't worry, we'll drill a new well."

"Mommy," Gary warned. "Gotta go potty."

The inside, my husband confessed, was unplumbed, except for an ancient toilet seat in a tiny closet that connected with a second-floor tank and a zinc cistern, which in turn was supplied with rain water caught off the roof — "a direct thrust system," according to the proud new owner. At the moment, though, there was no thrust, as the eaves had fallen off the house and the "cistern" was full of holes.

"So it's back to nature," I said, nudging Gary into the weeds. Only his head was visible above the crabgrass.

"It has beautiful lines, though, don't you think?"

"What?" I said, helping the child with an obstinate zipper.

"Four layers of roofing up there." He pointed to what looked like an undulating snake.

"That's good," I said.

"Well, no. That means they were too lazy to take off the old stuff. Just kept adding the new on top."

"Oh. Too bad," I said, watching the stream arc neatly out of the weeds and over a white peony bush.

"Wait till you see the inside," said Spence.

I helped the boy pull himself together, gathered up Lesley, and stepped warily across the shaky porch and through the door. Ahead of me, Gary shrieked.

"What is it?" I cried, plunging in after.

"See-saw!" he hollered, jumping up and down on the teetering floorboards, until a chunk of falling plaster cooled his ardor.

I found myself in a dark, low-ceilinged room heaped with

fallen plaster. In it a dead bird lay shrouded; a glazed eye stared up at us. When Gary picked it up, the wing came off and Lesley screamed. Spence lit a kerosene lamp, the only source of light. Overhead, the ceiling bulged ominously as though large objects might suddenly hurtle through the cracks.

"Old-fashioned plaster," Spence said cheerfully. "Made with horsehair. Don't find that around much any more."

"Really?" I said.

"No insulation, of course. Trouble is, they nailed the outside boards directly to the studs, so if the wind blows, it'll rattle the newspaper you're reading indoors." He chuckled.

"Oh ho," I echoed.

"But you haven't seen anything yet."

"I'll bet."

I followed him through the descending kitchen, with its cast-iron sink and lead drainpipe that went nowhere, and down into the attached woodshed, which had been "splayed off its foundation," he explained, by the '38 hurricane. In one corner was a three-seater outhouse, with splintered holes. The children disappeared into a sea of trash: tin cans, old shoes, newspapers — the residue of generations. He'd already taken two trailer loads to the dump, Spence admitted, standing knee-deep in what looked like another ten.

I peered through the crooked window frame at the forest of burdock, sumac, and locust trees that hid the mountains. You couldn't see the blossoms for the bees that swarmed around them. Through the underbrush a chicken house with a collapsed roof was barely visible. The last chicken had lost its head twenty-five years ago.

"Mom!" Gary cried, diving up through the trash with a red-plaid cap that he placed on his blond head at a rakish angle. "We gonna live in this broken house?"

"That's the plan," said his father, with a modest grin.

"Hoo-ray!" the child shouted, shuffling up to me in a pair of cracked rubber boots.

"R-ray!" Lesley echoed, her pink cheeks dimpling as she waved a pea-green beer bottle crusted with grime.

I smiled bravely and went in to use the outhouse, tugging the wooden door shut behind. Only it wouldn't shut. And a colony of bees hummed up out of the oval holes to greet me. So I stumbled outdoors behind the peony bush.

In my own space, I sighed, at last.

Once More unto the Breach: The Broken House

IT WAS A HOT, HUMID day in mid-August, with storm clouds massing in the North. Spence and I had rushed over from New Hampshire in time for the closing at the National Bank of Middlebury. He had completed a session at the university, where he was working toward a master's degree; the children and I were in muggy Andover, trying to dodge thirty summer scientists who kept up the nocturnal tattoo on our dormitory pipes. The faculty wife in my novel was still frustrated, but at the end of her tunnel a redhaired hero was to appear in a Rolls Royce and rush her away to greener climes.

The closing might have been a scene out of Dickens — or the Brothers Grimm. We were gathered in the office of chief cashier Peter Hincks, a tall, lean man in his sixties with a cranelike neck who took in the world at a glance. Behind him on the wall, Franklin D. Roosevelt and other bygone Democrats stared down at us, like extensions of the cashier. Their gaze made me uncomfortable, clad as I was in a cotton dress and no underwear at all due to a recent breakdown in the school washing machine.

Next to Hincks sat Charlie Adams, a taciturn man in his fifties and grandson of a former Middlebury College president, who served as attorney for both buyer and seller. On a hot day earlier that summer we had run him in circles between us with wheelbarrow, sand, and bag of cement, to knock in iron stakes and mark the property boundaries. Because there was only one actual marker, and the deed was fuzzy, we had to have it quit-claimed, with agreement coming from four neighboring property owners only after an hour of raised voices. The three acres "more or less" on the deed were definitely "less," coming down in the end to one and a half.

To me the chief drama lay not in the signing of the deed but in the presence of titian-haired Vivian and her estranged husband, a short, stocky salesman in a pinstripe suit. The pair came together in our company for the first time in a dozen years. I observed their averted faces with sidelong glances. What memories lay buried there, I wondered, what forgotten dreams? Might we be the catalyst for bringing them back together?

Just as their eyes at last turned to connect over the discussion of an outbuilding, Peter Hincks rose up between, and the moment was lost. Six months after the closing, Horace LeDuc did return to Cornwall — not to Vivian but to the cold embrace of the family cemetery.

We signed over our $250 in cash, shook moist hands all around, and walked out, dead broke but with a house that one day, according to the LeDucs, would become a historic monument — if only we could manage to resurrect it.

We raced the storm clouds south to Cornwall. One of them got ahead of us, dumping buckets as we scurried into the house with two quarts of beer and our new deed. Inside, we discovered, it was raining as well, staggering down in thin streams through two separate holes in the roof.

"Congratulations," I said, "we just bought Niagara Falls."

"Oh we'll fix a little leak like that in no time," insisted Spence, running to get an old aluminum pail from the trash shed.

"Tee hee," went a pair of swallows where they sat smug and dry inside a hole in the cornice work.

"Seal the roof. First job," Spence said, placing the pail under one of the leaks.

"You're doing it yourself? We can't hire someone so we can be in here by Thanksgiving?"

He made a show of pulling out his pocket flaps — Red Skelton, his favorite comedian, on Skid Row. There was a hole in one of the pockets.

I sank down on a wooden crate. I pictured the children grown, ourselves old and whey-faced while I handed Spence one more board to hammer over one more hole in the ever-leaking ship. For a bleak moment we sat watching the rain plunk into the bucket and then dribble out through an invisible hole in the aluminum bottom.

"But I'll have some help," he said, handing over a paper cup of beer.

"Me?" I said, recalling the night after an indoor football practice when I tried to fix a crooked leg on the horsehair sofa and it split apart.

He patted my shoulder. "I'll have help," he repeated, nodding. I imagined his ancestor Abel nodding in the same way as his hapless wife, just off the boat from England, surveyed her one-room log house and the pig wallowing in the middle of the puddly floor.

He did find help, in spite of the hole in his pocket. Not from his father, though, who had little aptitude for building and whose only offer was to touch off a match "and make an end of it." But he availed himself of a succession of local carpenters whose services to the Wrights had been handed down through the generations. There were Albert and Fernand Martin, a French-Canadian father and son. Strong workers, but short, they had to teeter on the top rungs of rickety ladders to put up the ceiling. The pair chattered in French as they ripped out plaster and boarded up the kitchen and living room. Most of what I could translate of their rapid-fire patois described a mythical fishing trip in the Canadian wilds. According to their gesturings the fish they brought home to their wives were the size of whales, and had put up a battle as fierce as Moby Dick himself (or the giant rabbit that later assailed Jimmy Carter down on his Georgia river).

And there was one-eyed Ed Matthews, whose grandfather had written a history of Cornwall. Ed knew the house so well that when Spence warned him of contamination from the water, he claimed he'd been drinking it for "well on fifty years, give or take, and I ain't worried now." Ed helped to seal the roof against rain and squirrels with forty-five-pound rolls of cheap roofing, and put on a new roof over the ell that constituted our kitchen. To accomplish this, the Wright-Matthews team first had to peel away the four layers of roofing that had been added after each major storm by old-time residents, resulting in a humping and billowing like the sea in the grip of Neptune's wrath.

Hunched over in faded denim, his good eye focused on the work at hand, hooked nose sniffing out the root of a problem, Ed talked continuously to his tools and the boards he was attacking. When they didn't cooperate, he upbraided them with a series of lively epithets. On Sundays or at funerals, though, he appeared in the Cornwall Congregational Church, the soul of sobriety in a worn black suit, to assume the role of caretaker, bell ringer, or chief mourner. His shoulders appeared to straighten on such occasions, as if he carried on in his single person the work of his grandfather, the Reverend Lyman Matthews, whose austere maroon tome of Cornwall's history, from its early "pitches" in 1774 to the heyday of Morgan horses and Merino sheep in 1862, took up a sizable space on our bookshelf.

As he worked, Ed would dispense choice tidbits of early church gossip, with sly glances at me and an occasional wink at Spence. Ed's father had hidden the old records in his grain bin after the church fire of 1914, and when Ed discovered them in 1946, a large number of pages had to be extracted from the mice nests. There was the tale of one Sister Douglas, for example, who was punished for allowing "vain mirth" and dancing on the occasion of her daughter's wedding. And the farmer who caused a new ordinance: "No Sap Boiling on Sunday," after he missed church one March Sabbath due to an overdrip of sap. But the tale that brought the most winks told of a long-ago Cornwallian who was accused of calling her husband a "cussed ole devil," and of threatening her daughter-in-law that if she came into the room, she would split her down with an axe.

"So, what happened to the woman?" I asked.

"Well, sir," said Ed, "They called her in. Wrote letters. Sent the elders to see her, but she never did repent. No, sir. So they excommunicated her (wink). Delivered her over to Satan, y'see? (wink). Poor husband was left in peace then (wink, wink)." Tucking his tongue into his cheek, squeezing his bad eye shut, Ed stuck a nail into a board and whacked it in with a blow of his hammer.

I imagined the grim-faced elders in black, branding the woman with a red N for Namecaller — and still she refused to give in. Her banishment to the presence of the devil, I decided, was nothing new: it was he with whom she'd been living all these years, and calling by name!

A new light was shed on the story when I discovered that Ed's own wife, after a few years of marriage, had "lost her marbles" and had to be "put away." Who was at fault and whether the two stories had any connection in Ed's mind, we never found out, although local legend attributes the breakup to Ed's mother's overprotection of her only son. If so, our sympathy must lie with the cast-off wife.

Ed was responsible, too, we think, for our first official visit from the local minister, the Reverend Wilder, who came to town after his former church burned. He didn't stay long, as his wife never "took" to Cornwall. He walked into our house one afternoon in early September, a few days before we were to return with the children to New Hampshire. A robust man in his upper sixties, he wore a blue serge suit and the ingratiating smile reserved for potential new members. Spence's mother, we told him, attended the Congregational church in nearby Middlebury, and we were married there. I couldn't say why she never came back to the church in her own town.

I was soon to find out. Accustomed to all conditions through his weekly parish visits, the reverend hardly blinked at the undone state of our house, and accepted a seat on a ladder rung and a cup of lemonade with good grace. We discussed the weather and the orchardists' latest complaints and the burning of his former church, which he described with glowing eyes as if Satan himself had gone up in it. And then Spence mentioned that his great-grandfather, Victor Wright, had once attended the Cornwall Church.

"Oh, you're *those* Wrights," said the reverend, who allowed that he'd been reading the old church records, and promptly veered off on a fresh subject: what did we think of a possible yoked parish with the town of Weybridge? (We looked at each other blankly.) A short while later he was on his way, shaking hands all round, patting the children's heads. But never a word about our joining the church.

"Why not, do you think?" I asked Spence that night as we lay staring up at a gutted ceiling that resembled the rafters of an ancient ship. It was our first night aboard — and alone; the children were "downstream" with the long-suffering grandparents.

"Well, it could have something to do with my father. No minister in Addison County has ever been able to get a foot in the door. Or maybe —," he chuckled.

"Maybe what?" I said, nudging him out of what seemed to be a private joke.

"Maybe it was because of Victor."

"Your great-grandfather?"

"Yup. He was thrown out of the Cornwall church for breach of promise. Over a century ago it was. A Wright hasn't dared go back there since. As kids, Mother dragged us to Middlebury to be christened."

"Breach of promise? How breach of promise? Tell me." I sat up, hugging my knees.

"Well, Victor Wright had a Merino sheep farm out on Mountain Road in northwest Cornwall. I took you by the cemetery where he's buried, remember? I showed you Petticoat Strip?"

"Mm. Silly name. Go on."

"Victor was pushing thirty and still not married. He was a big man — over six feet, red hair. He had five hundred acres of land and almost as many sheep. Sold fertilizer on the side. A real catch. At least two women panting after him."

"Mm," I said again, thinking of the redhaired hero who was coming to sweep away my beleaguered heroine.

"One was Marietta Foote, his childhood sweetheart. The other — Anna Mae, I think her name was. A widow in her thirties."

"Anna Mae," I said. Already the story was writing itself in my mind. "Anna Mae. There's a conniving, impoverished, desperate country widow for you."

"Right. Well, she wooed him with every trick in the book. Appealed to his stomach, his glands — you know." He turned to me, his blue eyes narrowed.

I elbowed him, and he went on. "Anyway, the poor fellow couldn't resist. She spread it all over town that they were engaged. Had the banns posted in the church. He didn't know what was happening."

"Goodness, no. Her little pinkie kept that six-foot man right in line."

"Do you want to hear the story or not?"

"Uh huh. Go on."

As Anna Mae pushed for a wedding date, Spence explained, Victor "ran scared." Sweet, shy Marietta began to bloom in his mind. One night he popped the question, then arranged a wedding date with a minister in Middlebury. When Anna Mae found out, she went racing over to Victor's barn, making such a bawling, Spence said (quoting his father, who got it from his father), "you couldn't tell the widow's noise from the sheep."

"Anyhow," he went on, "Anna Mae sued. For breach of promise. She got herself the best lawyer in town. Used all her feminine wiles. Wept and wrung her hands."

"Ha," I said. "Typical male-viewpoint story."

"Is it my story?"

"Go on."

"She won the suit. As settlement she was to get a portion of Victor's meadowland — of her own choosing. She wanted to pick it out right then, of course, but her lawyer said to wait until August when the corn was full. You could tell which was the most fertile part of the meadow, you see, by measuring the height of the stalks."

"So Anna won out. Aha — shrewd lady!"

"Wait. Story's not over." He gave a happy little chortle. "Victor didn't wait until August. It was May then. He and his hired man went over to the rockiest strip of land — by the Lemon Fair River, and dumped on a hundred loads of black, well-rotted manure, all ready for planting."

"The scoundrel!"

"August came, and Anna Mae and her lawyer marched over to

pick out her prize. Of course Victor made a big show of keeping her from the manured strip where the corn was a full foot higher than the rest."

"And she fell for it? I can't believe she fell for it!"

"Of course." He guffawed, his cheeks pink in the strip of moonlight that fell across our mattress. "Victor hung his head and pretended she'd done him in, while Anna Mae pranced off, grinning. The next spring, though, she wasn't smiling. The Lemon Fair flooded over and washed away the manure. And there it was: twenty acres of rock ledge. To this day they call it Petticoat Strip."

"The villain. He deserved to be excommunicated."

"He died a rich man," Spence said. "But at age forty-eight. Team of runaway horses pitched him over an icy ledge a couple miles from his house. He never woke up. Marietta and their son — my grandfather — sold the sheep and squandered the family fortune on a bunch of kooky investments."

"He would have been better off with Anna Mae after all. Just think: you and I could be wallowing now in all that rich manure."

"Yeah," said Spence. "We could pay off this mortgage."

"Outrageous, the whole bunch of you!" I buried my face in the pillow. I didn't know whether to laugh or cry. I didn't know how to deal with these rooted and unrighteous Wrights.

"It's all right," said Spence, misconstruing my noise. He flung an arm over my back and pulled me to him. We hugged together like ships coming into harbor. Upstairs in the undisturbed bedrooms the swallows cooed in their nests.

The next day I made it official. I went down to have a sign made. We hung it over the front door for all to see: THE BROKEN HOUSE, it read.

Spence, Ed, and I broke a bottle over it.

Recycle! Recycle!
Vita Breve Est

THE FOLLOWING WINTER, at the age of fifty-nine, Stan Wright died suddenly of a coronary. Middlebury "Deke" and classics major; World War I pilot and barnstormer; Knox Hat salesman; World War II naval lieutenant; and Director of Admissions at the college where he is still a legend — he lived lustily to the end. Only months before he died, he dumbfounded a roomful of college administrators gathered to discuss ("ad nauseum," according to Stan) the problems of coeducation and its aftermath, by rising up to announce that castration might help. The intervention of Yale President Griswold kept him from losing his post when the latter phoned the Middlebury president to offer "that forthright admissions man" a job, in the event he'd been fired.

Stan left me with one gift of advice. Two days before our wedding he had invited me into the college snack bar for a cup of coffee.

"Whatever you do," he warned, fixing my eye with his, like some ancient mariner, "don't keep all your pennies in the pot. It's an Ashworth trait. I see it in Spence — his mother's influence. Remember: Vita breve est."

Our eyes caught over the flowered rims of our coffee cups. I remembered his father, Albertus, whose unwise investments let the Merino Sheep fortune go to dung. Stan himself was always turning his pockets inside-out for spending money. And yet I believed his advice the way one treasures a deathbed homily or a mother's whispered warning in adolescence. I'd pass on the advice to my own children, at the same time reminding them of the Ashworth frugality that kept the family nourished through the Depression while Stan was pacing the streets in search of a job. The two views weren't wholly incompatible, I thought. One could both save and spend, recycle and take risks, without turning into a Jekyll-and-Hyde.

And recycle we did in those days. We were still teaching at Proctor, but spending summers and holidays at the Broken House. We were "camping in" that second summer. Spence had promised a room a year, but the schedule was erratic. He spent each morning in the college library writing a master's thesis on the unfought Battle of Crown Point — a fort on the "other" side of Lake Champlain that had burned down when a housewife's soap-making project boiled over. How he squeezed one hundred pages out of the subject I never knew, but he did. I typed it, three times, complete with footnotes that had a way of crowding off the bottom of the page and onto the typewriter platen.

By noontime each day the historian was at work gutting walls and chimneys, drilling holes in the studding to run wiring, and sawing out second-hand lumber for door frames. We were slowly moving from "broken" to "recycled" house. There were lumber rejects from the new college field house, cast-off window screens and shutters, old barn boards and beams — no elderly barn was safe from his marauding eye. In return, we had our own discards. Built onto the front of the house, breaking the classic lines, was a sixteen-by-eighteen-foot porch with two sagging steps — a "recent" addition. "It has to go," I said.

We boarded up the front door and nailed on a sign: PORCH 4 SALE. Automobiles shot past and then backed up. People climbed out to ask where the sale was. "Not PORCH sale," I told them, "Porch FOR Sale"; and pointed out the fine print: $40. U Remove It.

One hot afternoon I was heading north from Lake Dunmore

with the children in the back seat when Gary shouted "Mom! It's our porch!" And it was: perched upside-down on the back of a flatbed truck, its two steps ascending into air like a stairway to heaven, the handprinted sign still nailed to its railing. We waved, but the driver stared straight ahead, his face a stone. It was his porch now, he wanted no late bidders.

While Spence labored on the second floor, I operated down-stairs in the kitchen. We had a third-hand gas stove and a white enamel cabinet from the pantry of a distant relative, Vermont's then lieutenant-governor. (One Thanksgiving noon it crashed over onto the splintery floor, mixing oils and syrups with flour and spices, and like its former owner, was withdrawn from office.) There was a cracked sink with disconnected drains, and two sawhorses joined by a plank to hold a five-gallon jug-with-faucet. The latter constituted our water system.

The water was used a minimum of five times. Early each morning I pumped some from the shallow outdoor well into the five-gallon jug, which, with Spence's help, I heaved onto the sawhorse plank, where we lined up to perform our morning ablu-tions. "Bend over!" I'd shout at the kids. "Let the drops fall back in the jug!" Afterward the water was used for dishes, letting the rinse water splash into a bucket under the disembodied sink. This in turn served to rinse out diapers, and finally was dumped into the old unflushable toilet to swirl away the day's activities.

I managed to get the daily recycling operation down to two hours, twice daily; to put in an hour or two on Spence's thesis, and if I was lucky, an hour on my own novel. Jane Austen may have hidden her work behind her embroidery, but I'm certain she never worked on a wooden plank beside a bucket of soaking diapers. If my chapters opened on a sour note, there was good reason.

During the odd hours when I wasn't typing, cooking, wash-ing, soaking, or flushing, I was holding the other end of a beam for my carpenter husband, or aiming a light at some pulpy orifice. Only the dream of a lamplit armchair and a Victorian novel kept me spinning from task to task.

The water crisis came to a head the following Christmas vacation when we held our first party in the Broken House. For heat we were using two old kerosene heaters; wood stoves weren't so airtight in those days, and the dust and smoke tended to leak through and turn the cracks in the ceiling pitch-black. One stove we installed in the front "parlor," running the charred stovepipe through an enlarged hole in the ceiling and up through the center of the children's room above. The hole presented a problem for Santa Claus, of course, as the children had a grandstand view of the Christmas Eve proceedings. Santa had to wait until the wee hours of the night; then lie flat on the threshold of the room, and with outstretched arms, wiggle the dolls and trucks under the tree.

The second heater, in the kitchen, quit with a shuddering sigh moments before the guests were due. Spence was just up from his nap and dressing — it was his habit to sleep before a game, trip, or party, then emerge bright and rested while I clucked out greetings like a harried hen. It was ten below outside and a cool forty-six degrees inside. I'd have called off the party, had we owned a phone. Luckily, the first arrival was an engineer. He peeled off his shirt to embrace the sooty intestines of the stove, and the temperature soon rose to a sizzling fifty-eight.

"Coming," Spence called from upstairs. "Ready or not."

"Ready," I hollered up. "Thanks to your guests."

The homemade dandelion wine, though, did more to warm the blood than any heater. The more the guests imbibed, the more they forgot to observe the rules we'd typed up and slipped into pockets, according to sex, at the start of the evening:

MEN!
FOLLOW NATURE'S CALL OUT INTO THE GARDEN.
LADIES!
YOURS IS THE INDOOR HOT SEAT. DO NOT FLUSH!

I'd dump a bucketful of water into the toilet every twenty minutes or so. Even then I wasn't sure it would go down. The concrete cover Spence had cast for the cesspool was so thick he couldn't lift it to get at the pipes and assure an open passage. I nearly drowned a guest, the friend of a friend, who was squatting there in the dark. She muttered something about "everyone has a flush toilet these days," but soon swung into the mood of the evening with the rest: a round of shouting charades ("I dreamed I went to the Wrights' in my Maidenform bra"), and a frenetic hopping up and down in the name of dancing. At two a.m. they popped out into the chill night as warm and flushed as newborns.

Ruth Wright put her ark of a medical school on the market that winter, and by early summer had sold the building to a couple named Lane, who turned it into a tourist home. *Vermont Life* wrote up the place — a bit prematurely, as it folded shortly afterward, its assets "frozen," according to rumor. Before the sale my husband had hustled away several old doors and windows, some 1816 planking from under the house, and a few iron fixtures Ed Matthews had put in. As a bonus, most of the furnishings followed behind, including an attic-full of antiques bought at auction by my inveterate mother-in-law: spokeless spinning wheels, armless yarn-winders, wheelless wheelbarrows, seatless chairs. All of this, along with twenty-five years of *Better Homes and Gardens, Yankees,* and *Vermont Lifes,* was to be stored in our barn, while she retired to her lake camp to decide what to buy next.

My cheek quivered as I watched the truckload arrive. "Don't worry, it's not coming in here — yet," Spence comforted, but my cheek wouldn't quit. I imagined her Victorian antiques, some of them on casters, sliding down the slanted floors to the rear of the house and trembling together there with the passing of each oil truck.

I was in my seventh month of pregnancy that June. To me, happiness was a flush toilet and a bathtub full of cool water. Neither was on the immediate schedule. Since Spence's cousin Paul, a stocky, agreeable fellow, happened to be visiting the lake camp at that time, Spence felt the hour had come to jack up the rear of the house where it sagged a good sixteen inches below the anterior. Paul was familiar with the Broken House. He and his wife had spent a ski weekend here — aborted when their dog drank the anti-freeze in the toilet and had to be rushed to the vet's.

The jacking took place at night, with kerosene lanterns hung out the back windows. Using a borrowed ten-ton jack and groaning like Atlas holding up the world, the two men hoisted the house's weary backside a dizzy nine inches. Declaring it stabilized, they shoved wet cement in under the cedar post to form a footing, then retired to the refrigerator to celebrate their labors.

"Use the place any time this winter," Spence urged. And

couldn't understand why his cousin demurred, "guessing" they'd stick to the Waybury Inn.

Instead of a bathtub, that summer I was awarded an ancient and rusted shower retrieved from the Proctor Academy dump truck. With the pipes as yet unhooked, I stood while Spence drizzled a bucket of water over my clumsy flesh. We were to return to New Hampshire in time for the birth, but first there were other jobs on the agenda: the unborn child and I were low on the list.

My husband has only the dimmest notion of chronological time and none whatsoever of deadlines: Erma Bombeck might have had him in mind when she wrote of the housewife calling "Dinner!" to her husband at the improbable hour of three in the afternoon only to watch his feet turn automatically away from the table to start "one last job." Like a squirrel, Spence would store his nuts, one by one, in his tree hole until it was replete, in the vague knowledge that winter was on its way. In the case of the Broken House, the schedule of jobs must be completed without interference before the return to Andover for the opening of school.

"You'll be glad of it," he said, "we'll be that much further along when we come back here in August with the baby."

"Come back here?" I said, clasping my hands over my swollen belly where I'd struggled out of the "shower" and into a shapeless shift. "But we'll only have a few weeks before school starts. How can I bring a new baby here?"

He smiled indulgently and went on with his work of gutting the chimneys and heaving the brick and plaster out the window onto the back lawn for reuse "as a patio — I'll have you cooking outdoors by Labor Day," he promised.

Everything he did was to "make life easier" for me, he said. The next act of altruism was the removal of the three-holer in the trash shed to make room for the Skil Saw and lumber, and ultimately for "my" living room.

The next weekend four football teammates, all branded "brothers" from DKE — Willie, Bob, Tom, and "Ox" — arrived with their wives to share the Lake Dunmore cottage for a long weekend. "DKE Forever" they all sang, unaware that within months the Middlebury frat house would go up in flames one early morning, with coeds leaping out the windows like Rubens's flying angels —giving the president pause for the unheeded advice of his former admissions director. With his friends in hand, Spence declared a "Privy Day," and the brothers took up the cause.

A rock of Gibraltar made of tongue-in-groove lumber, the outhouse would be moved entire and carried a quarter of a mile down the slope behind our house to rest at the marshy bottom, where it would ultimately rot and dismember itself. A round of refreshment, and the brothers were ready to undertake the mission.

With the foursome gripping the corners and Spence giving a hand wherever a muscle flagged or a knee buckled, the ten-legged monster grunted slowly down the hillside. It had rained that morning; their legs were plunged into wet, waist-high timothy and vetch. The wives and children gathered around the old pump to watch, while I went down ahead as an advance guard.

"Just like shoving that ole dummy around, hey Spence? Nothing to it," said Ox, a 220-pound ex-tackle with a square jaw that had once quickened the pulse of the adversary. He held his corner of the privy aloft with a giant fist. Bob Gore, on the other hand, of slighter build and already the father of three, was breathing hard; while Tom Duff, who had lost a kidney in World War II —shot by mistake with his own revolver — was speechless, his cheeks blowing in and out, his Irish face scarlet from the exertion.

"How far we going?" panted Willie, a brown bottle poking out of his back pocket and no free hand to reach for it. He'd come to college at the callow age of seventeen to find himself rooming with my brother, a jaded Air Force captain ten years his senior. Together they operated a lucrative cash bar in their fraternity room.

I laughed — and then sucked in my breath. Several feet below the oncoming outhouse a single shining wire stretched across the land.

"Hey! Up there! Slow down! A fence!" I screeched. But they didn't hear; they were absorbed in some frat tale Willie was telling. There was a bellow of laughter. The three-seater wobbled in the air like a loose football. A roared command from Coach Wright brought them to their senses and the privy lifted, the goal in sight. Willie in the lead, our heroes plunged down the wet hillside:

"Christ!" Willie screamed. And again: "Christ! I'm being electrocuted!"

The men dropped everything. The outhouse crashed to the ground, pinning Willie full-length against the pulsing electric fence. His wet sneakers shuffled the grass, his eyes bulged behind the round eyeglasses.

Ox went to the rescue and then screamed himself. The shock went through the men like the chain reaction from an earthquake. It was only the bees swarming out of the three holes that got them moving uphill again, while Willie stumbled behind like a spotted leper.

The electric fence, Spence recalled later but never dared tell his band of martyrs, had been installed, with his permission, by the farmer who owned the pasture below our house. One or two of his herd had blundered up past our barn and into the road; the fence would curb their wanderlust. As it had curbed ours.

As for the privy, the children tried to make a hut of it, crawling in and out of the three holes, but for obvious reasons they abandoned the venture. Later they converted part of the wooden structure into a tree hut that to this day squats high in the notch of a gnarled apple trunk. The bees were unseated, but pine-scented spray and lemon oil have never been able to eradicate that "certain odeur."

"Look," I said to Spence, remembering his father's advice: "I want a brand new toilet. I'm sick of getting pinched every time I sit down. Some things you can't take with you, you know."

A month later our third child was born. We'd returned to New Hampshire only days before, the baby rocking low in my belly. It wasn't due until mid-August. But the date of August 7 was a powerful one: my mother had died that day on her way home from Scotland, within hours of my giving birth to Lesley. So three years later, on August 6 (just in case), nine children gathered behind our dormitory for her birthday — and voilà! that same night (aided, I think, by the ten little Indians) I went into labor.

I rode in style to the hospital, a pink paper birthday hat tied under my chin, and was set by the doctor to walking the grounds. Spence saw the event as an athletic challenge. Under his coaching we trudged sixteen hours and almost as many miles, around and around the country hospital. When the doctor disappeared at zero hour, Spence was prepared to go the full route, but happily, the former arrived just in time, breathless and cheery. He'd been off riding his horse (also named Nancy). Seconds later a red-haired, green-eyed boy emerged. We named him Donald Victor, thus bringing together my Scottish heritage and Spencer's Vermont stock. Donald's further adventures proved that he combines the most wilful genes of both.

Eight days after the birth we were on our way back to Cornwall with a new load of diapers and a third-hand toilet salvaged from a refurbished bathroom in our dormitory. Seated humming on the chipped porcelain, chin on his fist like a Rodin sculpture, blond urchin Gary blinked benignly through the rear window at the cars moving up behind.

"A chip off the old block," I said to Spence, winking back at the child.

Spence laughed where he sat in the driver's seat, his freckled hands holding the wheel as lightly as a fly rod. Between us our new son Donald lay in his car crib, his hair shining copper in the shaft of sunlight that danced in through the windshield.

"So. You're a pretty good recycler after all, you know that, Nance?" he said. And clearing his throat of the unaccustomed compliment, he zoomed us down the highway and on past the sign that read "Welcome to Vermont."

Who's That Knocking on My Door?

I SPOTTED HER TIPTOEING across the lawn, a plump elderly woman in a green print dress, a canning jar clutched in one uplifted hand as though she might hurl it onto the side porch and dart away again. Peering anxiously at the Broken House sign she retreated a step, then, sucking in her breath, she stepped up to the door and knocked.

It was Nellie Boardman, the shy widow who lived in the big yellow house next door. A "maiden lady" schoolteacher, she had suddenly acquired at the age of forty-six a well-drilling husband and five adolescent children. Alone again a decade later, she was still hanging enough wash on the line for a small army. Twice a day she reeled in and out, according to the weather, a variety of sheets, nightgowns, diapers, and long underwear. Then she'd hurry inside again, stooped under the weight of other people's washing, before I could catch her eye and wave.

And here she was at the door, thrusting forward a jar of crabapple jelly. She would have retreated at once if Spence hadn't dragged her, eyes popping, into the house. He sat her down on a narrow sawhorse, where she remained, still as a statue, one arm slightly raised as if to grab at the air for balance. He put a glass of lemonade into it.

"Do you folks ever go out?" were her first whispered words after Spence chattered on about his work in the house. The children squatted on either side of the sawhorse, ready to reclaim it for "riding" when the time came.

"It is nice to get away now and then," I said, thinking her on the verge of an invitation. Besides, I was curious to see her house. The Hurlburt House it was called, after Elijah Hurlburt, who caused our house to be built back in 1795 when he gave his daughter Clarissa and her intended, Fred Frost, a strip of land (an exceedingly narrow strip, I said to Spence). I knew Clarissa well: a slender woman with dark hair that staggered down her back like the weeping leaves of a willow. She haunted the dark corners of our bedroom closet (and often hid things on me). She'd lost two babies, I'd heard, and I liked to think she now had mine to watch over.

"Well — I could babysit," Nellie said in a burst of good-neighborly zeal that caused the sawhorse to tilt forward on its wobbly legs. I rushed to take her glass, and for a moment the two of us were caught in a heavy embrace. As she prepared to sit again, the sawhorse galloped away. It was Spence who came this time to the rescue, bracing her up from behind.

Giving a little giggle, she allowed that she had to be going anyway. She didn't renew her offer to babysit (eyeing the galloping sawhorse), or suggest that she take over our washing, but she did repeat the visit at least once a week — a loyal neighbor, with a fresh jar of quivery jelly borne in her two hands like a gift from the magi. Blueberry, gooseberry, huckleberry — the jars filled up our kitchen shelf. Always she would smile away our invitation to "sit," then fly off like a hummingbird when a knock came at the door.

One time the knock came from Helen Sadler, the Middlebury College president's wife — a handsome gentlewoman who, along with my mother-in-law, frequented a variety of clubs in town. She was dressed in tweedy suit and pumps, her hair freshly done. With her was her daughter Nancy, a dark-haired, unmarried woman in her twenties. They'd come for "tea," said Mrs. Sadler, gazing after the plump woman in sneakers who was at that moment dashing around the back corner of the house.

"Spencer invited us," she said.

"Oh. Do come in," I said. "The Sadlers are here," I called back
to Spence where he stood hunched over in his ragged shorts and
T-shirt, drilling holes through the studding in hopes of attracting
electricity. I smiled bravely. How many guests — bankers, old
school chums, plumbers, gas men, even policemen ("you never
know" is my husband's motto) — have we entertained at all hours,
in our nightshirts or BVDs, because "Spencer invited us!"

He ushered the women toward a pair of ice cream parlor
chairs my mother in law had recently acquired at auction. Of 1910
vintage, they had round white-painted rims but no bottoms. "Oh
you can always get that done," Mother Wright said as she carried
them in triumphantly. Mrs. Sadler didn't seem to notice, she was
exclaiming over the "large airy room. You'd never guess from the
outside!"

"It looks big because there's no furniture," I said. "In fact,
those chairs — "

Already she was lowering herself into one. "Ooh," she murmured. The perfect guest, just back with her husband from Arab
country where the teas might have three wives as hostess, she
wriggled her derrière until it overlapped the rim. Of lesser girth,
her daughter had to perch on the front rim of her chair, feet
planted wide, torso angled back to keep the chair legs safely on the
floor. The barest look of pain glimmered on her face as she sipped
her tea.

The visit was a success, though, as a third guest shortly
appeared: Earle Batchelder, a tall, blond colleague from school.
Nancy's eyes lit up at the name. The moment was electric as she
rose to press his hand and he pressed back. He was here to spend
the night, he announced, on his way north — "I promised Spence."

"I have a sleeping bag," he added, noting my dismay.

"Good," I said. "If you don't mind spreading it between two
sawhorses."

"Sawhorses, hell," said Spence, whose language always ripens
in the presence of friends. "We'll make a bed! I've got the stuff right
here." He popped open a beer, offered it to Mrs. Sadler, who
demurred; and then to Nancy, who put her lips to the can, her eyes
melting into Earle's over the gold rim.

The social afternoon flowed along, with an occasional pause

for Spence's drill or the rumble of an oil truck; but after Mrs. Sadler left, thanking us as prettily as if it had been a tea party at the Garden Club, it disintegrated into a bed-building bash. Nancy stayed on to hold up one end of the two-by-fours while Earle sawed them into bed rails. Together they dragged the crooked frame upstairs, where they alternately giggled and hammered.

And so a new romance sprang up in the Broken House. It culminated a few months later during a "South Seas" party in our side yard. We nibbled at bananas hung on the big maple tree, and drank out of coconut shells. Earle was devastating in a skirt made of sumac leaves. What happened between the lovers that evening I didn't witness, but it poured rain, and the next morning Earle's car got mired in the mud of our driveway. The romance seemed to sink with it as the couple glared at one another through the rain. Eventually Earle married a different Nancy, and he and the president's daughter ended up in separate bedrooms.

Three more beds were built in a hurry the day Spence's classmates, the Sullivans, arrived for a weekend in June that went on for ten days. We helped Jane Alice and "Sul" drag in four sleeping bags, two of them complete with kiddos, as they called their offspring, Becky and Beverly. Since the quartet was to stay only two nights, we were happy to share our water jugs, chamber pots, and refrigerator. The compleat Mother, June Alice had brought along a wicker basket full of dresses and undies, jars and bottles. We cleared a space on the top shelf of the refrigerator, labeling her jars with tape to differentiate them from ours. Lesley was delighted: she now had female playmates in the two girls, along with young Ann Collier, the doctor's daughter who had moved in next door. Put off by the predominance of females, Gary took to the fields to indulge in his favorite sport of chasing cows. Although we now had electricity, we were hardly ready for guests, with no water and only three half-finished bedrooms for the nine of us. But after all, it was only for a weekend.

Then the morning they were to leave, Beverly took sick. At first it was just a small fever — a cold coming on, we agreed. A little orange juice and aspirin, and she'd be fine. "Maybe we should stay one more night," said Jane Alice, a maternal wrinkle deepening in her forehead.

The next day the fever rose, the child developed spots. We called in Dr. Collier. It didn't seem to be measles or chicken pox as far as he could tell. He prescribed aspirin, an antibiotic, liquids. "We'll take a little blood sample," he said, "for good measure."

Our eyes were on the sick child when a crash sounded over in the corner. Spence, fainting, had pitched forward into the wicker basket, and its contents exploded like the aftershock of an earthquake. Poor Beverly was forgotten as Dr. Collier rushed to revive his new patient.

"It was the 'blood' that did it," I explained. "He can work with the wounded — but talk about it, he goes boom."

"Bed rest," the doctor ordered for his two patients, and departed, with a quick glance at the motley household.

The fever remained, although the spots subsided. It appeared to be a case of old-fashioned flu. Sul went back to work. He was a salesman for a pharmaceutical firm, and sent up boxes of samples for the wife and kiddos he'd left behind. Jane Alice rose to the occasion. No longer a guest but a Mother Fighting to Save her Child, she cleared the refrigerator of unnecessary foods such as butter and eggs, and drew a line of masking tape down the center. Her half she filled with medicines and liquids: orange juice, lemon juice, cranberry juice, papaya juice. The cans had a way of oozing over into our half. She moved Beverly downstairs to isolate her from Becky, and turned the living room into a sick room. There the child reigned like an Arabian princess from under a great tent that breathed fumes of Vicks Vapo-Rub and camphor oil. Our children were instructed to tiptoe in and out of the house. Above all, they were not to breathe in the direction of the sickbed, in case they imported more germs from the outdoors. Gary, in particular, was ostracized, for who knew what microbes the Holsteins had discharged into the dung the boy bore in on his sneakered feet.

The only relief during the ten days while we all played hospital was the coming of the Ice Cream Man. A tall, lanky fellow, at least six-four, with shoulders hunched from pausing in doorways, he came dashing up to the house one day, did a soft-shoe shuffle on the porch, and banged on the door, shouting, "Ice Cream Man!"

"Shush!" said Jane Alice. "There's a sick kiddo in the house."

"Vanilla chocolate strawberry chocolate chip aand-dd pistachio," said the Ice Cream Man. "Ninety cents a half gallon, you can't beat the price. I come by twice a week."

"We'll take one of each," said Gary.

"We'll take vanilla," said Jane Alice, "I don't want any artificial colorings. Her stomach can't take it."

"We'll take chocolate," said Spence. "Two half gallons twice a week. Make that a regular." He dragged out a pile of bowls, including one for the Ice Cream Man, who declined, smiling. He had other kids expecting him.

"Come back any time," said Gary, his father's son.

Four days later the vendor did — with the "regular." Beverly was on the mend by then, and the tent had been hauled down and folded into the wicker basket. The trio was still with us, though, for an extra day in case the littlest kiddo should come down with Something (years later she married into the family and came down with a little Wright). We bought three half gallons — one as a gift to the doctor's wife, who had tumbled a load through her machine when our car broke its tie-rod and couldn't make it to the laundromat. This time, we found a folded slip of paper under one of the cartons.

"If you have time to read this, read this," it began. "Of course it is another letter from the old Ice Cream Man."

It turned out to be the first of a volume of letters. Most days he would start back to the truck, then pause in mid-flight and stride back, as if he'd just thought of it, to slip his latest epistle under the door. A clown to the children, to us he revealed his darker side:

> Did you know I have been having trouble getting Ice Cream? The plant has been working at full capacity for weeks now but the hot weather has kept up. This is great for business of course and fills our pockets with money. Money is not a major item with me though, I have always worked hard and seem to have enough money to be happy. But prices are rising on everything, and with 5 children it just about goes around. I am sincere about paying my bills and just as sincere about working. I get very upset when I can't finish a route. Where I take all the pressure of a day's work is in the stomach. A nervous stomach is what I got.

"I am not saying I am the only one with nerves. You probably have a bad day now and then. Or maybe like me, you have a good day once in a while and bad days the rest of the time. It seems the longer I go on my routes the more difficult it is to be late. I spend more time explaining why I am late than I do selling ice cream. Did you know I start my day at 4 a.m.?

"You say I have too much to do. Don't we all? I have my routes so that I can make a living in the winter, this is important if you are in the Ice Cream business. When summer comes I try to take care of those who take care of me in the winter. But then I am called upon by a variety of summer customers which, if my day goes okay, I have time to do. I have always said I would sell anyone Ice Cream if they are sincere. I don't expect everyone to try to be jovial though, we are all built different. Some days when I appear so happy is when the pressure is greatest. I am out of space now but will get off another letter next week.

Your Ice Cream Man

We were waiting for the Man the day old Lute Buttolph came to tea. Actually, we were expecting a neighbor, Ruthven Ryan, a sandy-haired man of thirty who grew apples up on Cider Mill Road. The son of Cornwall's first lady of society and a British Colonel in the Indian Army (now deceased), Ruthven had been brought up in England, educated at Oxford, and then Harvard. He was to come to high tea, according to Spencer, who thought to warn me a whole quarter of an hour ahead. I was counting on the Ice Cream Man — my only other refreshment being a box of saltines and a hunk of hard cheese.

"He's late," said Gary. "He always comes at three-thirty."

"Never mind," I said. "It's not his fault. And don't you say a word to him. He has a nervous stomach."

"What's a nervy stomach?" said Gary.

"You'll find out one day. And don't mention that to him either. Just smile and give him the money."

It was a raw, windy, rainy day in March, we were here for spring holiday. At least, I told Spence, we could offer our guest a decent chair to sit in. We'd had bottoms put into the ice cream chairs, and only the day before, Ruth Wright's auction car had backed up to unload an overstuffed chair onto the porch. It had left a trail of foam and ticking across the floor as Spence drew it up to the heater for the occasion. The heater knob was turned on HIGH.

As it happened, Ruthven and the Ice Cream Man drove into the yard simultaneously. Moments later Ruthven dashed up to our porch, his glasses streaked with rain, his right hand clutching a black umbrella that threatened to uproot him in the strong wind. In his other hand was the familiar package. He was impeccably dressed in dark suit and tie, with fine wool socks inside the shiniest of shoes. We dragged him into the house, where he collapsed into an ice cream parlor chair like a paratrooper relieved of his chute.

"Piss-tah-chio," he murmured, delivering up the package. "It was all he could get today. He says it's half-price. Hardly his best. Oh my, what a frightful day."

"Has he got a nervy stomach too?" said Gary, pointing at Ruthven.

"Of course not," I said. "And don't point. Go eat your ice cream." In the kitchen I counted up the saltines. If I didn't take any, that would leave three each for Ruthven and Spence, along with a nip of cheese.

I found our guest still ensconced in the ice cream chair, polishing his eyeglasses. "Don't you want this comfortable one — over by the fire?" I cried, giving my husband an admonishing glance.

"His back," whispered Spence, on his way to the kitchen.

"It's my back," said Ruthven cheerfully. "It was a frightful season for apples. For cider, I should say. That's all they were good for, really. After that frightful storm last September — the hail, you know."

"Oh. We were away. But it must have been — frightful," I said. "Can I offer you some tea?"

"Oh, grand," he said.

"I've got it," said Spence behind me. He handed Ruthven a plastic mug, a Lipton's teabag tag dangling over the side.

"He might like a saucer," I said. "For his teabag."

"She went out and bought new teacups," Spence announced

to Ruthven. "Just for the occasion. And now I've blown it. I'll catch hell when you leave."

"You know better than to listen to him," I told Ruthven — as Ruth Wright had warned many a guest against Stanley's hyperbole, her blood pressure rising just the same. I slipped a saucer under Ruthven's cup. He removed the teabag with practiced fingers and squeezed it onto the plate of saltines I offered. Spreading a handkerchief over his wool knees, he balanced the plate on top.

"Sorry," I said, rushing a napkin to him.

The children joined us, squatting cross-legged beside the heater, each with a large dish of melting pistachio. "Don't you think you should turn down the heater?" I asked Spence. I never dared touch it myself; like a crotchety old dog, it might growl and turn on one.

But Spence was in his painting pants. Every second counted. "In a min — " he said, crouched over the baseboards, his fanny in the air, eyes an inch from the brush he was guiding along the edge.

We were discussing the Russian novel *Doctor Zhivago*, which had just come out. I'd wept through it twice. Ruthven, I discovered, was a voracious reader of Pasternak and Solzhenitsyn, and passionately concerned with the plight of the Russian dissidents. He was speaking of the need for some kind of international amnesty (the movement began two years later, catching Ruthven up in it), when the sound of off-key singing came up the walk. I glanced over at Spence. "Uh oh," his lips said.

"Have you ever met — uh — Lute Buttolph?" I asked Ruthven, interrupting him midsentence.

"I don't believe so," said Ruthven. "Is he involved with amnesty?"

Before I could answer, Lute burst through the door like a rain squall, skidding into the living room on a diagonal course as if he were maneuvering a steep slope. It was four o'clock, he was returning from town. He couldn't stay, he said, holding up a hand: "God's truth I can't. They're 'specting me back in the barn. The girls, you know."

"Paddy's there, isn't he?" said Spence. Paddy was the hired man, of sixty years. The Wrights and Buttolphs shared a past. The older generation had been college classmates, the younger had hung out together summers when Spence worked on the Buttolph farm in Shoreham, doing chores and milking cows when the machinery broke down. Which it had this same afternoon — the reason, according to Lute, that he was in town. He was getting parts, and while he was at it, stopping in at the local grog shop. He knew a fellow who worked there, he said, didn't want to disappoint him.

"Why, so Paddy is," said Lute, his eyes connecting with a bottle of spirits Spence had left above the sink. He gripped my hand, and then Ruthven's; the latter rose to the occasion, his plate clutched in his left hand.

"By God, that heat feels good. It's a bitch out there," said Lute, sinking into the upholstered chair, still in his coat, his nose red with cold, and something else, too. He was at that in-between stage, I judged, where the rain and wind had begun to temper the alcohol. If I could get a cup of bracing tea into him, it might tip the balance.

It seemed I might. "What's that you got there?" Lute said to Ruthven.

"Lipton's, I believe," said Ruthven. "Lovely flavour. She's put some kind of lemon in it."

"I'll take mine with Seagram's," said Lute. "Fact is, I got some out in the car." He struggled up again but Spence waved him down.

"Never mind," he said. "There's some here on the shelf, with your name on it."

"Well, fancy that," said Lute, with a little chuckle.

"Have you read *Kon Tiki*?" I asked Ruthven. "My sister gave it to me for my birthday. It's fascinating."

"Not yet," said Ruthven. "But it's on my list."

"Found my teeth, you know," Lute hollered back to Spence, spreading his lips like a horse about to chomp an apple.

"The theory," I said, "is that the Polynesians came to the coast of South America millenia ago. Or vice versa. Borne along by the equatorial current."

"In the Cornwall swamp," said Lute. "Ole china clippers."

"From Asia to Peru," I said. "Imagine!"

"The next day, no less," said Lute. "Right where I lost 'em." He grinned at Ruthven and me.

I gave up. I knew the story. He'd been watching an American Legion ball game. His team lost, and on the way home from the consolation party he took sick on Swamp Road just beyond the covered bridge and lost his teeth in the process.

"Mabel went back with me. She was the one found 'em. Right where I spilled my cookies. Much obliged," he said with a wink as Spence brought in his "tea." "Require it for my arthritis, you know," he explained to Ruthven.

The latter bit into a saltine but couldn't seem to swallow. It sat there like a lump in his cheek.

"Anyone for pistachio ice cream?" said Spence, who had just discovered it.

"The heater?" I reminded my husband, who was helping himself to a bowlful after his guests declined. "Poor Lute will be cooked," I said. Already the essence of cow was beginning to ooze out as the wool dried on his coat. The children had retreated to another room.

"Don't touch a thing," said Lute. "Feels goddamn good."

"Have you tried aspirin?" said Ruthven.

"What?"

"For your arthritis. Aspirin. My mother swears by it."

"Only one cure I know of," said Lute, chugalugging his tea.

The afternoon wore on. Spence brought Lute a second cup, and then, on request, a third. Ruthven had one more Lipton's. He seemed determined to stick it out, a stubborn smile on his lips —like his father, no doubt, as he led a charge of the British army against the hordes of ragged Afghans.

"Lute went to Middlebury. Class of 1911," Spence said, trying to establish a rapport between the guests. "He was a Deke."

"I never joined a fraternity," said Ruthven, peering at Lute over his glasses. "But they're jolly good fun, I'm sure."

"Lute's wife was a Phi Beta Kappa," I said. "In mathematics."

"Really?" said Ruthven.

"She counts chickens now," said Lute.

"Ruthven's a pomologist," I informed Lute, hearing my voice a little shrieky. "That is, he grows apples. He has a lovely orchard up on the next road. He spends his spare time reading and traveling —don't you, Ruthven?"

"Well, the truth is, I'm about fed up with the apple business," said Ruthven. "So much dependence on the weather. And you're in farming I gather, Mr. Buttolph. Dairy? Beef?"

Lute's face under the thatch of silvery hair was the color of burgundy. The cup was tilting in his veined hands. The vapors from the heater made the room wobble in my vision. I could imagine the alcohol steaming inside Lute. I only hoped he wouldn't lose his teeth again, at least not until after Ruthven left.

Then Lute got up, swaying a little on his feet. The odor of Holstein was ripe on his coat. The cup waved in his hand as if he would lead a band, his lips trembled with what he had to say. I was apprehensive. I had heard from Spence about the latest Deke reunion. One by one the old grads had risen to sum up their lives: "I'm the president of the Marble Savings Bank." " I run a little stockbroking business down in Schenectady." "I'm chairman of the school board. We just built a million-dollar complex."

Then it was Lute's turn. . . . I could only hope that he would not give the same answer this time, but he did.

"Well, sir, I pull tits for a living," he said, and giving a little bow toward Ruthven, collapsed back into the chair.

Spence turned down the heater at once — but it was too late, Ruthven was up on his feet.

"It's been a delightful tea party," he said, reaching for his umbrella. "But really, I must be going now."

THE SHOP

To know the change and feel it . . .

John Keats, 19th century

Make Your Own Change —
Proprietors Out to Lunch

WE ARRIVED IN CORNWALL one winter afternoon to find Ruth Wright's car backed up to our barn. The door was wide open. Ed Matthews was at the entrance, bent double under the weight of an old pine sea chest — his head waggling in protest.

"Go on!" Ruth yelled out the car window. "Put it in there anywhere. Spencer will make room for it."

"Spencer will *not* make room for it!" her son hollered out the window of our gray Ford. "Spencer has other plans for that barn."

"Well, hello! I didn't expect to see you over here this weekend," she said. "What plans?"

"It was a nice day. We decided to come. And a good thing we did," he said, opening the back door to let out the children and animals.

"What plans?" she repeated. "You're not going to use that old wreck for anything, I hope. Anyway, I'm glad you're here. I've made up my mind. About buying a new place, I mean. I'm not: I can winter in Florida, summer at the lake. And there you are. I'll need your place to store a few things." She turned to shout at Ed: "If it won't fit in the barn, take it in the house." Ed backed out into the snowy driveway, his breath coming in gasps.

"No, don't take it in the house, Ed!" yelled Spence.

"Jesum," said Ed, and let the chest slide off his back into the snow. He sat down on it, arms folded, to wait until the argument was resolved.

Spence stepped around the chest and into the barn. Constructed in the last century and containing some twelve hundred square feet, the building had come to us complete with a second-story hayloft and two horse stalls. The signatures of its builders were still scrawled in the south corner, "Frank Brown: AD 1876" among them. The grease from the Model T that had superseded the horses was still thick on the floor. But it wasn't the grease that caused the look of dismay on my husband's face.

"I can't believe it," he said, staring in at the packed space. "And none of it belongs to us."

I stepped in behind him. The top floor was jammed to the rafters with Ruth Wright's paraphernalia. The bottom floor was taken up with a neighbor's baggage trailer, my nephew's sixteen-foot motor boat, and octogenarian Virginia Graham's Chevrolet from down the street. (Our barn was the perfect storage place for her "machine," she'd informed my mother-in-law, and drove it right in, denting the rear wall as she came to a sudden stop.)

Now there was the sea chest.

The freckles on my husband's face were the size of cabbages. If he didn't have a plan yet for the barn, he would come up with one.

"It's a lovely old chest," said Ruth. "See? It has the original initials: P.T.W. It was the W that made me buy it. I was thinking of one of the children. I mean, one day — "

"Put it in the barn, Ed," said Spence. And as Ed got up, he added, sighing: "But it's coming out again in May. Everything's coming out. This is a three-month warning, okay? You can tell the neighbors."

It was my brother Don who set the plan in motion. On a visit to New Hampshire, he and his wife, Mary, stopped in at a small shop in New London called Pinecraft House. They came back, both talking at once: "He makes his own stuff. Guy by the name of Henry Pogue. Beautiful work. Harvest tables, benches, hutches —"

"Braided rugs," said Mary, who hadn't been allowed to buy one.

"Those come from Massachusetts," said Don. "But wait till you see the pine chest he's making me."

"I don't need to," said Spence. "I already have one."

He went down anyway, one day after hockey practice. And came back as Henry's "partner." A personable man in his thirties, Henry had gone from Princeton into department store retailing in the Midwest. Years later he returned to New London to set up his own shop. Chairs that required special turnings, lamps, rugs, linen towels, and other such items he bought from established wholesalers, but the colonial furniture was all his own. His specialty, a handsome wooden hobby horse, was not only for sale, but on display in Concord with the League of New Hampshire Craftsmen.

"His partner?" I said. "And you've only just met him? And you've never built a stick of furniture in your life?"

"I have too," my husband said. "Where do you think these bookcases came from?"

Together we gazed at the largest of the three he'd built back in college. The top shelf sagged under the weight of Victor Hugo's collected works.

"Well, I couldn't help it if it warped, could I? Wood's as fickle as woman," he said. "Henry said that," he added quickly.

"I don't know about this Henry."

"Anyway — about the partner business. Henry has problems with his asthma, so I'm going to help him deliver stuff now and then. To New York City, places like that. And pick up new items on the way. You can come with me."

"Thanks."

"Things Henry doesn't have time to make," he explained. "We'll buy the stuff together. Only our shop will have a different name, of course."

"*Our* shop?"

He glanced at me, and started humming — the Deke marching song, a little off-key. "What do you think I want that barn cleaned out for?"

"Ah," I said.

In late April, Spence and Fernand Martin took off the barn's sliding doors and put in a picture window. It wasn't until May, though, when the pair started to yank up the floor planks, that the neighbors "got the drift." The sea chest was filled with old magazines and carried upstairs with the rest. The boat went permanently out to sea. And Virginia Graham came to get her Chevrolet. "What about the rain?" said the octogenarian lady. "My machine isn't used to it."

"Try an umbrella," Spence advised.

He went to work with a vengeance, hoping to hang his OPEN sign by mid-July. The floor planks were turned over and renailed, greasy side down. Underneath, some two hundred greenish beer bottles had come to light, along with a variety of blue and white patent medicine bottles. Alcohol had been the basic ingredient in most of those tonics. How many nights, he wondered, had old Frank Brown spent "working" in his barn, while his daughters scrubbed and knitted in the kitchen? The bottles were among our first merchandise; we priced them from fifty cents to a dollar, and at that the customer got a bargain. In general, the markup was low on everything — "you can't expect 'em to pay the piper in an old barn," Spence said — except for some cheap wooden tomahawks bought from an itinerant for ten cents and sold for twenty-five cents. On the strength of that outrageous profit the shop would soon pay for itself, he reasoned. And then we'd take a Real Vacation — just the two of us, he promised.

To Paris, I said, and sighed. Though I wasn't packing my suitcases just yet.

By the second week in July the cobwebs and hay were removed from the studding, the floor sanded and lacquered, and the walls sprayed a pale yellow. We poured a concrete step outside the door and hung a green and white sign: CORNWALL CRAFTS. We'd picked the name out of dozens suggested by friends — such as WRIGHT'S WRECK or OLD BARN BORED AND RUIN — for its solid and alliterative sound. If we couldn't make a go of it, we agreed, we'd change it to RUTH'S REJECTS and sell off the upstairs, at least.

The cement was still wet due to damp weather, so a plank led up to the open doorway as our first customer pulled in. It was late in the day. A black Buick with a Virginia license plate sped past, then squealed its brakes and backed into the driveway. Spence was down back mowing weeds. I sent a child after him. I was at a table by the window, typing a final draft on my novel. *The Cruel Mouth of Love*, I called it, after a line in a poem by Baudelaire. I was planning to submit it to the Bread Loaf Writers' Conference, in hopes of getting a scholarship.

A woman slid out of the car. She was attractive, smartly dressed in a blue suit. She gazed about her, took a deep breath. I saw it through her eyes, as Spence had envisioned it that first day: the rustic barn and the flowers I'd planted in front, the old house with the split-rail fence Spence had put up that summer, the smooth stretch of grass on either side, the doctor's roses. Beyond, the range of Green Mountains, like mounds of pistachio ice cream heaped one on top of the other — not a bad simile, I thought, and wrote it down.

Shouldering her pocketbook, the woman stepped bravely up the plank and into the shop. She'd walked into Colonial America, she discovered; its one room contained thumb-back and Governor Carver chairs, Boston rockers, a hobby horse, a large open hutch, a five-foot pine harvest table, an old pine sea chest. This last was the only antique, she discovered — no — except for a pair of old clocks on the wall, their pendulums wagging in restored rhythm. A pair of display tables held a variety of smaller items: wooden trays, bread boxes, boot racks, bowls, towel holders, cutting boards. And something that resembled — what? She picked one up. A toma-hawk, for heaven's sake? Well, she didn't need that.

But everything so inexpensive. Ninety-eight dollars for a handmade harvest table? Impossible! At home it would be double the price. She examined the table more closely. Fine workmanship. The table she had now was on its last legs. She was expecting her brother-in-law, the judge, for a visit — she'd have to have a dinner party. Would it fit in her car? Where was the proprietor?

"Yoo-hoo," she called. "Is anyone here?"

"Yes, ma'am. Can I help you?" said a tall redhaired man, still breathless from his dash up the back hill. His forehead was ruddy and glistening.

"You're the proprietor?" she said, looking down at his blue

shorts, patched at the front seam and starting to rip again. The bony freckled legs ended up in dirty white sneakers with black, double-knotted bootlaces.

And when he nodded: "Well, I'm interested in that harvest table. Is there anything wrong with it that it's priced so low?"

"No, ma'am. Though it might be stuck to the floor. We've just moved everything in, you see. It rained up until today, and the lacquer didn't dry the way I'd hoped."

"I'll take it then," she said quickly. And wrote out a check. He didn't ask for identification, but she gave the name of her brother-in-law, anyway. "Judge Douglas. William O. Douglas," she enunciated.

"Oh," said Spence.

"O. Douglas, yes. The Supreme Court?"

"I know," said Spence. "Let's go and measure your car, okay? And if it won't fit, even with the legs off, we can always deliver it."

"To Virginia?"

"Why not?" he said, with a generous spread of his hands.

Two more customers appeared that opening day. One was a woman in her forties with something that looked like a Great Dane on a leash. "Are you a native Vermonter?" she asked.

Satisfied that his family had filled a few local graveyards, she tied up the beast and came inside. She piled up some eighty dollars' worth of merchandise, and since there was no counter, laid it out on the floor: toast tongs, cutting boards, shaker pegs, salad bowls, Bennington mugs.

"At last. Made in Vermont," she said, turning them over.

Spence totted it up on his pad while she peered over his shoulder. Then she took a turn, and came out with a different figure. A third customer came along — a man, attracted by the Great Dane. "I've always wanted one. Are they friendly?" he asked, keeping a careful distance. He was invited to add up the tally. His result fell somewhere between the earlier two.

"That's it, then," said Spence, cramming the things into three recycled A&P bags.

The fourth car came at 11 p.m. The place was still lit up. Spence had a beer in one hand and a paintbrush in the other when a

New York car pulled up and four heads swiveled in the direction of the shop. "You still open?" they shouted.

"C'mon in," said Spence. And they did: two laughing couples, headed back to Ticonderoga after dinner and a movie in town. Although it cost him four cans of beer, Spence earned another $23.35. When one of the women took after her husband with a tomahawk, he at last announced it was closing time.

"One hundred ninety-seven dollars and fifty-five cents. Wow!" I said, with visions of the Eiffel Tower.

But Spence's face only reflected gloom as he surveyed the shop. There was an empty space where the table had been. The display tables were visibly diminished. "If they keep buying it up like this," he said, "what am I going to do? Henry's in the hospital —another asthma attack."

"You'll have to have more space, that's all," I said. "To store things in. Then, when you sell one of something, you can rush another right in."

"Oh yeah," he said, his eyes lifted to the upper loft. "Oh yeah."

"But no more tomahawks," I warned.

He nodded.

The next day a band of young Indians sprang up along Route 30. Shrieking with glee, they scalped everything in sight, from the tips of cats' tails to the new rosebush I'd planted in the back yard.

OPEN 7 DAYS A WEEK: 9 TO 9, read the Cornwall Crafts sign that we'd hung on a pole out by the road.

"What about your mother's dinner?" I asked the first Sunday after we opened the shop. Sunday dinner at Lake Dunmore was at best a five-hour affair, served at 2 p.m. on the outdoor picnic table after much rattling of dishes and running around after the right plates and silverware. I was usually too crammed with roast beef and baked yams to take a swim afterward, but the children enjoyed it. Ruth ate alone most of the week, and it would break her heart if we didn't go.

"No sweat," said Spence. "We'll go."

"Right. We'll shut the shop then."

"Who said anything about shutting the shop?"

PECUNIA, he labeled an old salt box from Ruth's auction attic. MAKE YOUR OWN CHANGE. PLS WRITE DOWN PUR-CHASE, he scrawled on a piece of cardboard. For that purpose a pad of paper was left beside the salt box, which he stuffed with pencils and assorted change. Vermonters never locked their doors, he reasoned, so couldn't his shop run on the faith system?

"What'rya, crazy?" said Lachlan Field, an artist-friend from down the road who was carving an eagle sign to hang over the door. He'd arrived that first Sunday to measure the space, and looking for a pencil, had stuck his hand into the salt box. He pulled out a wad of green stuff. "I was a nervous wreck, for gozzake," he complained. "Creeping around like a thief, and nobody there!"

Each Sunday noon after that we'd take off for Lake Dunmore, leaving behind only the cat — the shop doors wide open, and the salt box perched on the end of a display table. Each evening we'd return to a flood of scrawled messages.

The Sceptic: This is some kind of joke? I could steal you blind.

The Enigmatic: We were here. Mort and Minnie Drawbridge.

The Opportunist: I loved the shop but couldn't find anything I needed. But I took five ones for a five.

The Defensive: I put in a ten-dollar bill and took out $5.60 for a whale cutting board and a red candle. THAT WAS ALL WE TOOK!

Spence's Uncle Mortie Hemenway, a retired cake-decorater and artist whose roots dug humorously into rural Vermont, began a series of cartoons for the shop. One of them depicted an oversize lady (he'd married into the Ashworths) ploughing out of the shop toward the car, where her husband waits — her hand stuck in the salt box. "But, Horace," she's wailing, "I only wanted to see if there was still any salt in it!"

In spite of its gala opening, the shop operated at a loss that first summer — and no wonder: the proprietor and his wife were busy with other pursuits. Spence submitted the final draft of his thesis and was awarded his M.A. from the University of New Hampshire. In mid-August a letter informed me that as someone had dropped out of the running, I was now a Bread Loaf Scholar — the only "unpublished" one. I found the air rare and heady up on the mountain, and for two weeks played the role of Young Writer with a Future, while Spence and the children wore on down in the valley. To my surprise, Jealousy reared its freckled head, as Spencer kept appearing in the middle of lectures or readings to lure me away to Cornwall. "Just for an hour," he'd beg.

"Hush," I'd say. "That's Robert Frost reciting up there — can't you hear? 'Love and a Question'?"

"That's what I'm afraid of," he'd say. "C'mon. I'll read you the poem at home. Just for a little while. Okay?"

"Oh, all right," I'd say. "But this is the last time." And we'd slip out together, into the dark.

We ran into Robert Frost again that summer, on the day of the biggest shop sale of the season. We'd left the children with a baby sitter to attend the outdoor wedding of Polly Upson, the daughter of William Hazlett Upson, famed for his Earthworm Tractor stories in the *Saturday Evening Post*. The Upsons had the camp next to ours at Lake Dunmore. When Spence was in bed with rheumatic fever at the age of nineteen, William Hazlett had read to him daily in his high squeaky voice. Spence literally laughed his way back to health. On this occasion, though, the author radiated dignity in his father-of-the-bride suit, and it was his friend Robert Frost who gave us a chuckle as he stood beside us at the refreshment table. He wore a faded blue shirt and worn sneakers; his shock of white hair rumpled in the breeze.

"I loved your reading, Mr. Frost," I said. "Up at Bread Loaf. We met the last day, remember? When they took our pictures?"

"She never heard the reading," said Spence. "I dragged her away. I needed her more than you did."

The poet chuckled as he munched on a sweet: "If I hadn't been the one up front, I'd have left, too."

"You know," Spence whispered, nudging me with his elbow, "He's got smarts — for a poet."

"That's more than I can say for you," I hissed back, "embarrassing me like that." But he just laughed.

We arrived home to find Donald squatting on the shop steps, a grin on his round face. He'd sold the big hutch cabinet. They were coming back the next day to get it. "I told 'em it was the best one in Vermont," said the three-foot salesman, pulling a rumpled check out of his pocket.

He'd been building blocks in the driveway, he said, when the big car drove in. The others were down back in the field. The people asked where Mommy or Daddy was, and he said he was in charge.

When the customer carried the hutch out to the New Jersey station wagon the next day, redhaired Donald was on one end, along with his father, the apple cheeks blowing in and out with pride and pressure.

"All right, now," Spence said to his mother at dinner the next Sunday. "About that stuff up in the barn. I'll give you nine months to dispose of it. We're planning to expand next spring. Upstairs. And if you don't get rid of it — well, you know who will."

"You're crazy," she said — a woman who'd learned to deal with a maverick husband and three male offspring — and dug contentedly into her mashed potatoes.

If We Don't Have It, We'll Invent It

WHEN THE SPENCER WRIGHT menagerie departed on Labor Day for New Hampshire, Ruth Wright and Evelyn Wright McGregor moved in. "You shouldn't leave a shop alone like that," my mother-in-law said as we carried in her antique spindle bed and the trunk full of fall clothing. Popping a candy into her mouth, she unpacked four bulging boxes of "staples" brought up from the lake, along with ice cream, pastry, nuts, and her favorite butterscotch candies. "An empthy houth invithes trouble," she warned through the butterscotch. "And ith thilly not to keep the shop open for the leath peepthers."

So began a new era of shopkeepers for Cornwall Crafts. While Ruth settled into the empty house like a nesting bird, her sister-in-law, Evelyn, Stan Wright's only sibling, kept shop. The pair hadn't gotten along since the day Ruth excluded Evelyn from her bridal party because (according to Evelyn) she was too plain and skinny. The truth was, Evelyn said, "the rest of 'em were too fat — they looked like tugboats struggling against the tide!" Evelyn was as angular and spare in speech as Ruth was round and expansive. Evelyn smoked and drank like a snowbound Vermonter; Ruth was a purist. Evelyn wrinkled her long nose at housework and clothes while Ruth took pride in her homemaking, although by the early sixties she was already inclined to sit and read *Better Homes and Gardens* and let the debris heap up around her.

A Vermonter transplanted to the acrid soil of New York City, and for thirty-five years the only woman working in a Greenwich Village typographical union, Evelyn called a spade a spade, a fart a fart. In the mid-forties she married a short, solemn Scotsman known as "Mac" McGregor, a proofreader for the *New York Times*. Together they built a house in West Nyack and commuted into the city. Five years later he died in a city rooming house. Evelyn, always herself, continued to play poker on the daily commuter train and throw back her head in a deep-throated laugh when she won the ante.

Ruth took over the cooking, kept the shop books, and rocked in her chair while Evelyn sat by the window to keep vigil for an out-of-state car. When one came, Evelyn rushed to greet the customers before they could get out. Their eyes popped at the sight of a "native" Vermonter, her skirt hanging over the long underwear she put on each Labor Day, the gray hair in ragged wisps around the long face, a grin on her lips below the feathery mustache. Only when she ushered them through the open doors into a converted horse barn did they take their eyes off the "proprietress." If they were buyers, they found Evelyn willing but foxy. There were to be no discounts, she made clear, they were to take things as they found them. When a woman inquired about a hobby horse that had one green eye and one silver (substituted after the original was lost), Evelyn told her: "So? They had different fathers." She sold the shade off an apothecary lamp, and later the lamp itself, with a mismatched shade, assuring the customer that there was one just like it in Calvin Coolidge's house. "He wrote all his speeches under it," she said.

If the customer wasn't a buyer, just wanted an excuse to use the toilet or water a dog or baby, she told them to go ahead into the house but to watch out for her sister-in-law, who distrusted people, was apt to grow "violent — she's only been let out to visit," she warned, her sharp eyes glinting behind round wire glasses. Ruth later complained that people would rush out of the toilet "without even a flush or a thank you!"

The one thing Evelyn never let on to people, and even to herself, was that she was painfully nearsighted, hadn't had her prescription changed in twenty years. Asked for a second set of blue placemats, she might slip two green ones of a different make into the bag. We did a lot of exchanging of goods by mail over the course of the winter.

When the last yellow leaf wobbled off the trees and the leaf peepers went home to Brooklyn or Eastern Suburbia (to the re-leaf of Vermonters not engaged in tourism), Evelyn locked up the shop and went with them. For years we tried to entice her back to her native state on a permanent basis. But home was where your cat was, she maintained, and hers happened to be in West Nyack.

She lived alone until the age of eighty-six, along with her ancient white cat, Frumpy. We'd go down several times a year to clean out the house and raise a glass of scotch with her. One morning we found her on the floor, waving her hands and legs like a beetle on its back. Full of scotch after an evening of storytelling with Spence, she'd tripped over the cat and spent the night there —"too blame lazy to get up," she said as we hoisted her onto her feet, bruised but laughing.

But if we'd ask when she was coming "home to Vermont," she'd narrow her eyes like an old fox. Waving at a roomful of faded photos, portraits, shabby furnishings, and the green-and-silver-eyed orphan horse she took back one autumn, she'd say: "Hell — I got all the Vermont I need, don't I? Right here?"

The next summer we gained, through an act of fate, a new shopkeeper to help out Sundays and mornings while Spence, still waiting for the barn loft to empty out, hammered the shed into a living room for the Broken House and I attended the Middlebury French School, laboring toward a master's degree. Being female, I wasn't allowed to teach English at Proctor Academy, but when one of the male language teachers was discovered holding hands with a student, I was invited to join that department.

I was seven months into a fourth child (a redhaired girl, I told everyone). And we had a new well — dug into the roots of my yellow rosebush — that gave us one and a half gallons a minute during the winter months when we weren't there, and usually managed to dry up during the heat of summer when we were. We were still taking off for Sunday dinner at the lake. The "make your own change" system was working out quite well, we thought, but evidently one of our neighbors disagreed.

One hot Sunday in July we came back to find our neighbor Virginia Graham's short, broad body filling the Boston rocker we kept out front, her long earrings swaying with the motion of the chair. She was dressed up in a red-flowered chintz, a matching grosgrain ribbon tied in a bow on her two-toned hair (rising up from the center of her silvery head was a thickly coiled brown bun, made from her own hair a quarter of a century before).

"Ah'm tending the shop," she said in her Virginia accent. "You all can go on into the house." Planting her cherrywood staff between her feet, she thrust up out of the chair and shuffled inside the shop to advise a pair of perspiring ladies how to lighten the heavy purses they bore over their shoulders.

Of course we had known we would find her there one day or another, the way Mary Poppins was not wholly unexpected each time she dropped into one's world with her umbrella. If Virginia's "machine" was banned from the barn, her presence lingered on. A southern Daughter of the American Revolution, she had migrated north through a series of self-run tea shops and restaurants, bringing little beyond the clothes on her back and the box of family silver that had lain buried when the Union troops swarmed through the ancestral homestead. We never knew just how true the story was of her grandmother's inviting the "bluebellies" to a succulent dinner and then sweeping the whole feast — china, glassware, roast pig and all — onto the floor with a tug of the tablecloth. But we could see that Virginia lived by its example. A gutsy, resourceful woman who left her husband ("Mister Graham") because, she said, he objected to the dressmaking "sweat shop" she was running in a back room of the house, she ultimately established the Cornwall Guest House down the road from us, then sold it again to convert the 1830 sheep barn next door into a Swiss chalet. THE BARN, a weatherboard sign announced on the lawn; and on the front door: VIRGINIA GRAHAM, in bronze. Although she rented out one floor and took in "old" people to care for (herself then in her late seventies), it wasn't enough. From the moment the CORNWALL CRAFTS sign went up over our barn door, her green eyes narrowed with purpose.

And so she watched the shop on Sundays and opened up mornings. Spencer was a "B" person according to Virginia, in contrast to herself, an early morning "A." He started the day late and slow, gradually accumulating energy until he reached a frenetic pace in the evening, dashing about house and shop, hammering and hollering until well past midnight. He was quite content to let Virginia take over until noon.

Wedged in her rocking chair, needles flashing like Madame Defarge knitting the names of French Revolution victims into her work, Virginia rarely missed a sale. Who dared move past The Presence without a purchase? She told the customers what they wanted to hear. You want a cherry end table? Why, sure, honey, we make cherry. An oak bookcase? Of course! Everything's oak-kay! People would arrive weekday afternoons while Spencer was tending shop in his work shorts and demand to see the owner; "she" had told them that CORNWALL CRAFTS could build anything.

"Now what we want," they informed the redhaired shop clerk, "is an octagonal table in sandalwood with Queen Anne legs, and . . . "

Virginia convinced browsers that a pine chest was yellow birch ("same principle," she said) and they hauled it out; sold them "unbreakable" linen towels when they came looking for china to send to Aunt Minnie. She sold a copper lantern we'd hung for display and charged extra for the fly specks: "That proves it's old," she said. She sold a customer the very rocking chair she sat in; when asked for a discount because it had been exposed to the weather, she rose to her full five-foot-three (topknot included), gazed meaningfully at the place where she'd sat — and the buyer hurried to pay the price. If a purchaser wanted something shipped she flung up her arms and cried: "Why, Ah should say so! We ship anywhere in the world! Mah man will see to it."

"There has been a slight change of policy," her "man" wrote that winter in his surprisingly voluminous shop correspondence: "we can now ship only certain items — to certain places . . . "

Virginia even had customers believing she was a Vermonter in spite of her southern drawl. "Mah granddaughter was born right here in Burlington," she declared, filling them up with the details of her life. Virginia had already appeared in two books. Her daughter Ann Rollins, a former actress, was married to writer-critic Edmund Fuller, who had published, among other works (including a history of Vermont), *Successful Calamity*, the story of their family's migration from New York City to a Shoreham farm on the shores of Lake Champlain. A young couple with three children, the Fullers had expected to make the move alone. At the last minute Virginia decided to go along, and opened up a guest house on the premises, which she ran with the same persuasive hand she did Cornwall Crafts. When her daughter almost died a few years later, bearing a stillborn child, it was Virginia who took on house and children, and told "that doctor" a "thing or two" about women.

One August Sunday we arrived home at five o'clock to find the yard crawling with people. They were lugging out bags and packing up boxes. Dogs were barking and mothers shrieking: "Watch that old well, Harry!" "Keep out of that shop, I said, Rose!" Panicked, thinking we were being robbed — or worse, sold out, and Henry in bed again with asthma — Spence bounded out of the car to elbow his way through the crowd in search of his shop lady.

He found her. On the side lawn between house and shop, where she'd set up card tables. The merchandise, though, was unfamiliar. There were boxes of shoes, mostly size 5 (Virginia was a compulsive shoe collector). There were thirties-style hats, scarves, dresses. Faded curtains, rugs, kitchenware, a chipped toilet seat. Back isues of *Vogue* and *Life*, and several copies of *Successful Calamity* — autographed by Virginia. Thrown in here and there, a kind of tokenism, were linen calendar towels and Bennington mugs from the shop. A pink polka-dot ribbon nodding on her head, Virginia peered up at Spencer and then left him for another customer when she discovered he didn't want to buy anything.

She saw nothing amiss. After all, the shop had been remarkably dull that afternoon. What better way to attract customers than through a yard sale? "Ah called everyone Ah knew to bring things," she told us later when the crowd and the merchandise began to thin out. "Well, you all know what happens as well as Ah. Cars attract cars. It's a basic business principle." And tossing her head, she went on selling a ninety-cent pair of flowered bathing trunks to a Long Island woman with as much equanimity as she might have sold a set of salad bowls, had the shop been more lively that cloudy Sunday afternoon.

She could cope with any crisis, it seemed, even one of an intimate nature. Spencer and Charlie Willson, an elderly man who became Ruth Wright's helpmeet after the death of one-eyed Ed Matthews, were out front one afternoon, measuring for the long-threatened shop addition, when Virginia strolled past in a cotton sun dress. Her knitting bag flapped at her side, the cherrywood staff swung in her hand. She paused to visit. She and Spence argued politics for awhile — her conservative Democrat against his liberal Republican — and then discussed the size of the shop addition. She wanted more space. "A lot more space!" she cried, flinging out an arm. "Why this all is nothing but a pig in a poke!"

The conversation drifted on to the plans she'd made for our daughter's education: in three years' time Lesley must be removed from that "dreadful male bastion" we taught at and chipped off to Emma Willard. She'd get a "proper upbringing there, at least." All the while, ignoring Virginia, old Charlie Willson, who was hard of hearing, kept up a muttering dialogue between himself and his measuring tape.

The discussion swung back to local Garden Club politics and became a monologue: "And the new president doesn't know a peony from a peapod — her gardener does all the work!" Virginia's arms gesticulated, her foot stamped the ground. Spence glanced down, and then looked again, with horror. Something pink and silky was beginning to wriggle down her legs. He tried to look away, but each time her shrill voice commanded his attention, her bright eye riveted his.

"And there's that ole Greenburg — " she shouted. Greenburg was a New Yorker who'd bought up the apple orchard across the street from her barn. She claimed that his dust-air spray was crossing the road and killing her iris. "Well Ah called him at six o'clock this morning to demand mah rights and they said he was already gone to work. Work, huh! He was prob'ly lying in bed. But

Ah'll fix him. Tomorrow Ah'll call at five!" She laughed wildly and stamped her foot again. As she did so, the pink "somethings" slid all the way down to land in a crumpled heap at her ankles.

The freckles stood out like strawberries on Spence's cheeks. Old Charlie was struck dumb. He switched his tobacco chaw to the other cheek and stared in fascination.

"Five o'clock!" she repeated. "Ha, ha! That'll get the old fox out of his burrow!"

"Virginia," Spence murmured.

"He'll replace every single iris. Every one. And keep that killer spray on his own side of the road! Or Ah'll sue. You'll see if Ah don't!"

"Virginia," Spence said again. "You've, uh, dropped something."

There was the slightest pause, a lowering of lashes. The barest glimmer of pink in the cheeks. Then, like the flick of a snake's tongue she stepped out of the panties and hooked them up with her staff. With a quick "thank yaw," she stuffed them into her knitting bag and went on with her diatribe against Greenburg, the iris slayer.

It was Virginia's idea, of course, that Cornwall Crafts be included in the Garden Club's Old Homes Tour. "A 150-year-old barn! Original floor boards! It's a must!" she told the committee. Although a place of business was somewhat "irregular," they gave their consent. But then they agreed to put her barn on the tour, too, and in the end, Virginia deserted us to stand there in nineteenth-century costume, a pair of partridge feathers aflutter in her topknot. She left Cornwall Crafts to the elderly Lane Sisters, Jessie and Marguerite, who lived down the road. Maiden ladies and former schoolmarms, they boasted an ancestor in common with their "boyfriend" Spence, and argued in his presence over which of them he liked best. They nodded this time at his instructions, then ran the shop the way they wanted — as a tour, with no hint of the crass commercial. Their uncle had once owned our house; he'd lived there for a decade between Frank Brown's death and his own, in 1917. The sisters were quite at home.

"An historic site, our barn!" they proclaimed, curtseying in long skirts and white bonnets. "And here we have the original signatures of the builders. Over here, see? On the wall. Notice that the proprietor has carefully painted around the names so as not to disturb . . . What? Oh, no, we're not selling anything here today. Gracious, no!"

Virginia was horrified when she heard. After all, she herself had made a good profit on the day. When a visitor admired a small hooked rug on her bathroom floor she sold it. And the shop tour had been her idea to increase sales. "It just proves you can't trust other people!" she hollered the next morning when she swept into the house to bang on the stove grates and waken Spencer. She thumped a box of cornflakes down on the kitchen table (I had already left for the French school, maternity blouse clinging to my sweaty belly). "And especially stick-in-the-mud schoolteachers who've never known the business world!"

"Oh, Ah don't mean you," she said, softening her voice when Spencer staggered into the kitchen in his pajamas. "You all teach economics, after all."

Somehow the summer ended, the tourists departed, and Aunt Evelyn arrived back in Cornwall to take over the shop — or so she thought. We loaded three kids, a dog, cat, and rabbit into the old station wagon and headed for New Hampshire. It being Labor Day, and myself over eight months pregnant, I cautioned Spence to veer away from his favorite shortcuts and keep to the main road. We arrived, my belly still intact, and the next day established the older two in school. On September 22 I began my French classes at the academy. For the first time in my maternal career I was leaving nothing to chance. On the night of September 26, with my doctor's consent, I would go into the New London hospital to "start up the works." On September 27 a substitute would take over my classes for a period of two weeks.

I waddled in that first day, enormous with child, my cheeks ballooned and scarlet in front of twenty adolescent boys, most of whom were new to me and to French. Quelle introduction! I handed out twenty sheets of assignments. They fell into a panic at once. But how delighted they were to learn that I would go on leave after five days. When the time came and I said "au revoir," my face on fire, they sat there awkward and creaking in their seats, some with foolish grins on their faces. I heard later that they were disappointed I'd escaped the betting game. The school nurse, an entrepreneur like Virginia Graham, ran a pool on which day a pregnant wife would "break through." I'd taken the sport out of it by planning in advance.

The father-of-the-child managed to miss the whole affair. A player was injured in a football scrimmage at Tilton Academy, and Spence ended up in the Franklin Hospital at the precise hour of my delivery in New London.

"Is it a girl?" I gasped as the baby slid out.

"Why, so it is," said the doctor.

"Red hair?"

"How did you guess?"

"A redhaired girl," I repeated later to my husband, feeling as ingenious at my wish-come-true as Virginia Graham when she willed all wood to be maple, or oak, at the customer's fancy. "Anyway," I told him, "I've named her Catharine Wallace, after my Scottish forebears. You weren't here, so your side lost out this time."

He offered me one of the cigars he'd bought and said it wasn't a bad name, "not bad at all."

"No, thank you," I said to the cigar.

Later that week he brought along a letter from Mother Wright. After the congratulations and a welcome check for "the latest little redhead," there was the following news:

> Evelyn wasn't too pleased today. She trotted out to the shop to greet a male customer and found Virginia already there. The pair got to quarreling over what the man should buy for his wife's birthday, and when they turned around at last to consult him, he was gone. Each said it was the other's fault that they'd lost a customer. Of course Virginia followed Evelyn into the house trying to get in the last word.
>
> Well, I happened to be reading in the paper about how old Amos Butterfield had just died, and that put a new bee in Virginia's bonnet. She went on telling how she wanted her ashes strewn around the yard at her place — on her flowers and vegetables — while I said I wanted a fancy

monument in the cemetery and a lot of singing at my funeral. Evelyn naturally just sat there, smoking like a chimney (you must take out more fire insurance, Spencer, SOON!) and refusing to say anything until Virginia asked her point-blank: "Well, Evelyn? I suppose you all planning to be buried in your own cigarette ashes, is that it?"

Well, Evelyn just peered over her glasses and said, "You two go ahead and bury yourselves however you want. Only thing I'm dying for is a glass of scotch." And she got up and fixed herself one. Virginia followed her into the living room, still arguing, and I had to go out when the next car came. It was the same man, back again for his wife's present — he'd gone home to ask what SHE wanted — and then Evelyn and Virginia were both furious, because I'D made the sale!

And so the merry-go-round went, the three strong-minded widows hanging on for dear life to their separate horses, and each in their turn grabbing for the same brass ring. When it came Virginia's time to go, a decade later, her ashes were brought to us, fulfilling the promise of Ann and Edmund Fuller, to be scattered, with Spence's assistance, over her Cornwall flower beds.

And the bronze VIRGINIA GRAHAM plaque that had governed her front door was affixed by the Fullers to the old cherry-wood staff and hung over the doorway of our shop, where she had sat so many summers, flinging up her arms and crying: "Lor-r-dd, yes! We can make you all a zebrawood horse with purple eyes if that's what you want. Why, Ah tell you now, we can do just anything here at Cornwall Crafts!"

Henry Was Here

THE PILE OF "ANTIQUES" in the barn loft appeared to be one of life's contradictions: the more you took out of it, the higher it grew. We found out why one day when Charlie Willson was discovered tiptoeing up the shop steps with a huge wicker basket that Spence had given to the firemen's bazaar only days before.

"All right, Spencer," his mother said. "But I found this basket at the bazaar — it's exactly like my other one! They're more valuable as a pair, you know."

"Mother, they'll be carrying me off in a basket if we don't get this junk out of here," her son moaned, putting a hand to his chest.

"Good," she said. "Come on, Mr. Willson, we can start filling up the downstairs again."

The Battle of the Bulge at an impasse, Spence turned with a sigh to the living room: it needed a proper foundation. The three-holer removed, along with much of the old shed, the floor was propped in the rear on three timbers. He contacted the job service for a man to pour concrete.

The next morning Henry Swider appeared. A man of stocky, athletic build, with black hair and keen blue eyes, Henry went straight to work. In three days he poured all the footings and revolutionized Spence's schedule where Virginia Graham had failed. If Spence wanted Henry, he had to be ready to go by seven each day. A coffee break?

"Well, okay, Spen-sah," he said in his clipped Polish-American accent, "but make it short. When I work, I work. We can talk on our lunch break. I take up to nineteen minutes. No more. Okay, Spen-sah?"

"Okay," said Spence, overcome at all the work getting done.

Hired for three days, Henry stayed thirteen years — leaving in the end only to start up his own surveying business. Educated by Polish nuns in Webster, Massachusetts, Henry spoke better Polish than his Polish-born parents, who insisted that their six offspring be brought up "American." He built the family a house with his own hands, splitting up eighty-five massive stones for the foundation. It was his passion for fishing that brought him to Vermont. He landed a "beauty" when he met dark-haired Mary on the shores of Lake Champlain.

During his nineteen-minute lunch he held us in thrall with war stories of his Polish relatives: his grandfather, who ran an underground press; his aunt and cousins who were marched away by the Russians to Siberia. "Swapped" a year later for his uncle, they were put in a concentration camp by the Gestapo. When one of the boys escaped, the aunt was mercilessly beaten. Yet she survived, Henry said, and lived to be ninety-eight years old. "A strong lady," he said in one of his typical understatements.

One day an insurance man, stopping by the house, told a Polish joke. "Careful," said Spence. He pointed at Henry, up on a ladder, hammering in a board.

"How does a Pole change a lightbulb?" the man brayed, beginning another joke. "Well, it takes one man on a stepladder and four more at the bottom to turn the ladder!" He laughed uproariously.

"Very funny," said Henry. He leaped down to confront the man, the hammer raised in his hand: "Now go ahead and tell us a joke about yourself!"

Most of the stories, though, involved Henry's own experiences in the war. Chief signalman on the heavy cruiser USS *Baltimore,* he took part in eleven Pacific invasions. Spence made everyone who came to the house hear about the time the *Baltimore* carried President Roosevelt to meet with General MacArthur and admirals Halsey and Nimitz. "I never in my life saw so many five-stars," Henry would say. "My arm nearly dropped off trying to salute them."

But his eyes shone brightest when he told how he was one of four selected to take FDR and a boat full of Secret Service men fishing up in Alaskan waters. "I reckon that was the biggest one I ever pulled out."

"What about Mary?" I asked.

"She wouldn't like it if I called her the biggest," he said.

But after eighteen minutes and fifty-five seconds he'd glance at his watch and tell his audience: "Well, Admiral Wright here's going to fire me if I don't get back to work." And he'd slam his hammer down on the nails: bang! bang! bang! as if they were so many Japs or Gestapo or Russians he was pounding, as his mother's sister had been struck two decades earlier, during "The War."

One morning in the first week of Henry's reign, Virginia Graham came over to pound on the stove grates and waken Spence. To her astonishment she found him already at work with Henry. She rose up on her pointed toes, green eyes glinting under her beribboned topknot to see "this new man." She recognized him at once as a kindred spirit, a fellow "worker." With Henry, she decided, she could go far: landscape her barn, create an Eden of herbs and flowers that would make the garden club swoon with envy. First, though, she needed a new foundation under the house. For that she'd hired a succession of cut-rate carpenters, none of them, she claimed, "worth his salt." She never thought to equate the low pay she offered with the carpenter's productivity.

The day she saw Henry carry in a refrigerator on his back with barely a grunt, she knew she had to have him.

She dragged out a lawn chair, plunked it down where the men were working. Her needles flashed in the sun, her tongue flew as fast as her fingers. She wanted to know all about this Henry. When he didn't answer, being off-break, she filled in his silence with her own life: "When Ah was a girl down in old Virginia," she'd begin, "Ah loved to plunge mah hands in the spring earth . . ." Gradually she led up to the work she required.

Henry decided that day that he didn't need a coffee break.

Nine minutes was enough for lunch. He bolted down a ham sandwich and went back to his hammering.

"Earthwork," she cried as she clomped after him. "So what's Spencer paying you, anyway? Well, whatever it is Ah can do better. Ah'll give you two dollars an hour!"

"Spensah gives me two-fifty," said Henry.

"Two fifty-five then!" said Virginia. "You all can't better that! Just give me two days a week, that's all. What you and Ah can do to that place! The sky's the limit."

"That's what I'm afraid of," said Henry.

Wary of Virginia's earthworks — "You and I know, Spensah, it's just the old pick and shovel routine" — he paid Gary a dime each day to warn him of her approach.

"Where is he?" she'd demand, sweeping into the area where Spence was working: "Ah just want him to see what needs to be done. Maybe spade up the garden a little. Won't take but a minute."

"I'm sorry, Virginia," Spence would say. "But he's gone. You can see for yourself."

"Gone, mah eyebrow! His car is right there in the driveway. You can't fool me." Clutching her knitting bag, she'd march around the back of the house hollering "Hen-ry? Hen-ry! You all come here now!" She'd arrive at the front just as Henry's head poked out from around the corner of the shop.

"His car wouldn't start, Miz Graham. He got a ride home with a customer," Gary would say, fingering the dime in his pocket.

"Well, you tell him Virginia Graham was here. And she'll be back!" And she'd stomp off to her thwarted earthworks.

Although Henry never succumbed to Virginia's wiles, he did work for a time for her son-in-law, who built a small place down the road. He showed everyone the autographed copy of *Successful Calamity* that Edmund Fuller gave him. "A jewel," Edmund had written of his carpenter on the flyleaf. After we left for New Hampshire in the fall, Henry would stop in now and then to lift a cup with one of the shop ladies, Virginia or Evelyn McGregor. Reminded of the earthworks, he'd say, "Oh too bad. I got on my best shoes. Some other time maybe." And when Evelyn tried to lure him down to repair her West Nyack roof with the promise of free scotch: "Oh geez, I'm picking apples this fall. Over in Shore-ham. That's as far south as my blood can take."

What Henry didn't tell her was that Mary, his wife of six years, was dying of cancer. He didn't want to be too far away. "I can't talk about it," he'd say when the subject was broached. "Let's get to work, Spen-sah."

Winters, Henry worked for Bill Buzzell, a flamboyant general contractor with a fiery temper who extracted a maximum of labor for a minimal wage: a dollar-forty an hour, a nod for overtime. "Wild Bill," Henry called him; the man was still scarred from his first day on skis, when he drove straight down the mountain, yodeling away, and crash landed in a grove of trees, causing a small avalanche. "That's his mentality," said Henry.

He'd been working for us several years when Wild Bill, angry over a difference of approach to a certain job, abused Henry with a series of epithets: "You goddamn Polack!" he screamed.

"Whadyou say?" said Henry. "What was that word?"

"I said you're a goddamn Polack!"

"Say that once more. I want to hear it again," said Henry. Pinning Wild Bill under the arms, he lifted him up off the ground —though the man outweighed Henry by fifty pounds — and shook him until his hair stood on end. "Come on, say it once more!" Henry demanded.

"You're — fired," the man gasped, the eyeballs rolling back into his head.

"Good," said Henry. "That's the kindest thing you've ever said." And picking up his tools, he strode off, whistling.

Having no children of his own, Henry adopted ours, especially the oldest. "Round 'em up, Gary!" he'd shout as the boy raced after the hapless heifers in the field behind our place: "Don't let 'em get away!" In the winter, when the heifers were in the barn, Henry took Gary ice fishing on Lake Champlain. The pair sat patient as cats stalking a mouse; the ice shanty was stocked with beer and coke, cigars and ham sandwiches; the fishermen's lines dangled through the hole in the ice. At the end of the day Henry would take his share home to Mary. An outdoor girl before her illness, she took as much pleasure in the catch as her husband.

One March day Henry swung into the drive to shout that his shanty was sinking and he needed Gary to help pull it out. The nine-year-old rode with Henry to the rescue. A foot of soft snow had lately fallen on the ice, and the temperature was a balmy 40 degrees. The pair tiptoed across the slushy ice, Gary with a rope around his waist. "But what'll happen if *you* go under?" he asked his friend. "Forget it then, Gary," said Henry. "Just swim for shore."

The ice held, although out in the middle Henry's shanty was tipped forward into open water like a sinking *Titanic*. Henry tossed Gary another rope. "Lasso it now," he said. "Don't let it get away!"

According to Gary it was his rope that caught the shanty, brought it, heaving, up onto solid ice. Tugged by the two fishermen, the runners hissed along the ice and up to shore. The pair rode into our yard that evening, soaked and laughing, the shanty tied on top of the car. Gary's eyes shone like the moons of Jupiter.

"Wild Bill Hickok rides again!" he shouted.

"Don't say that," said Henry. "Please don't say that."

We were short of funds that spring. Our combined salaries seemed to disappear at once into the mouths of four children. Henry was working "on promise." Spence had appealed to Peter Hincks for a bank loan to finish off the living room and begin the shop addition. In the interim he and Henry would build a hut down back for Gary, made out of an old pole barn from Leicester Four-Corners. The barn was theirs for fifteen dollars if they would take it down. Armed with cables, ladders, crowbars, wrecking bars, Spence and Henry resembled Don Quixote and his squire Sancho Panza about to attack the windmill. First they wrenched away the old boards. Mounting ladders, they pried loose the timbers, one by one, with the four-foot wrecking bar. Some of the timbers were thirty feet long, weighing up to six hundred pounds.

"Watch out! It's getting away!" Don Spencer would shout.

"Run, Gary, run!" cried Sancho Swider.

Crash! went the timber on the sod floor, raising a dust that filled the fortress and got the knights to sneezing.

A week later they had the barn down, the timbers loaded into the farmer's wagon. For an extra ten dollars his herdsman would drive it to Cornwall. Off they lurched, Gary and Henry riding the timbers, Spence driving behind in the old station wagon, jammed to the roof with boards and tools. The herdsman swiveled his head back and forth as he drove:

"Hell — I took down a bigger barn 'n this 'un," he bragged. "Down to Salisbury, last spring. Man, I was ridin' them beams from the roof down. Y'mean it took two of ya to topple this 'un?"

"Three," said Gary.

"Sorry, son, didn't see ya there behind them big ole beams." Guffawing, he went on with more tales of his prowess.

But when it came to removing the beams, the heroic herdsman wasn't around: "Gotta go. Awful bad," he said, and disappeared into our bathroom, appearing only as the last timber was hoisted out of the wagon.

"Here you, Hercules, catch!" said Henry as he finally emerged. The man blanched at the sight of a huge beam ready to fly at him. In seconds, he was in the wagon and careening off down the road in what Henry called "the fastest move that gasbag ever made!"

The hut was completed and Gary moved in: baseball bats, army men, plastic pistols, skates, marbles, beer can collection. Building came to a halt. We owed Henry three months' pay and we couldn't ask him to do more. Goodro Lumber company would extend credit, but sooner or later must have its due. Town taxes, too, had gone up. In an impassioned protest to the Cornwall Board of Listers, Spence wrote:

> The Wright residence has been in a state of disrepair for twenty years, and in a state of repair for eight years. The above conditions still exist in the residence, despite the efforts of the present owners.
>
> Not that this will in any way affect my taxes: but I do not intend to leave town. I like Cornwall, have liked Cornwall, will always like Cornwall; and intend to maintain a residence in Cornwall until I am buried within its confines.
>
> Sincerely yours,
> Spencer Victor Wright

Spence made another appeal to the bank. Would Peter Hincks like to come down on his lunch break and see what we're doing? He had a good worker, he told Hincks over the phone, but couldn't afford to keep him. He had a shop losing money because of inadequate storage space. And he was thinking of starting a small tree farm, on some property his mother was about to turn over to him.

The bank officer came. I fixed a lunch of wine and cheese, Spence's pea soup ("Mmm," said Hincks). The two men ate and talked of the weather, the state of the economy — every subject, it seemed, but the Broken House. Meanwhile, Henry was doing his part. He gave up his lunch, made such a racket shoving the same board through the saw again and again that the lunchers had to raise their voices to compete. He marched round and round the house, hammering on the clapboards. Out in the shop, a neighbor dashed in three times to purchase the same bucket. Spence had to excuse himself to make the third sale, as I was rushing back to French class.

"Busy little place," the bank officer remarked.

"Oh we're going places, all right," said Spence. "Five hundred dollars would have this shop on its feet. With luck, we could leave teaching in a year or two, afford to run it full-time."

"Good worker," said Hincks as Henry appeared in the window, red-faced and sweating. A frenetic pounding ensued that rattled the banker's plate.

What clinched the deal in the end was the arrival of a fifth party. A plaintive "yoo-hoo" sounded, and then a scarlet hair ribbon nodded in the door window. In one hand was the cherry-wood staff, in the other a shovel. She was dressed in a pair of shapeless dungarees, a red bandana around her neck.

"Come on in, Virginia," said Spence. "Have you met — "

"Oh, yes," murmured Hincks, whose bank held her safe deposit box, complete with buried silver.

"Ah'm not looking for you," she said to Spencer, her voice breathless. "It's Henry Ah want. Mah foundation is caving in. He's the only one can fix it."

Henry's head appeared in the window, and she charged out. "Henry? Aha, Ah've got you now. You all come right on over this minute!"

"Come down to the bank tomorrow," said Peter Hincks. "We'll work something out. Five hundred won't be enough, will it?

Maybe a thousand?" And just as Virginia's hand was closing on Henry's shoulder: "Oh, Mr. Swider? I have a roof needs fixing at my place. You wouldn't be available some weekend now, would you?"

The summer labor on the new living room culminated in a party: a "painting party" we called this one. It was the third in a series of "living room romps." To this one we invited a dozen couples; Spence mixed up a "painter's punch" in a five-gallon paint bucket. On arrival each guest was given a brush, painter's cap, apron, can of white latex, and assigned a section of wall. "You mean, we're really going to paint?" said one woman in dismay, peering down at her pink cotton dress.

At first they took their task seriously: squinting at the wall with great concentration, applying the paint with meticulous care. "They're too serious," I told Spence. "They'll get bored. There's no chance to socialize."

"They're too sober," said Spence, and ran about the room urging a refill.

At ten o'clock the pink lady came to say good bye. "It was a lovely party," she said, one side of her mouth falling as she surveyed the ivory inroads into the pink of her dress.

"I like it," I said. "It's a kind of polka-dot. But please don't go," I added, running after her with an onion dip. "We'll stop painting soon and have fun."

"Sorry," she said, moving firmly out the door. "It's the paint fumes. They get to me. My allergy. Another five minutes and I'd be flat on the floor."

"The fumes," I said to Spence. "You never thought of the fumes." A curious off-key singing was coming from the living room. Someone raced past, giggling. It was Ann R. Painted on her derriere was a game of tic-tac-toe. A man was running after, paintbrush in hand. But it wasn't her husband, I saw, but Allen M. "You see?" said Spence. "The party's picking up."

Tom Buttolph dashed by, on his way out the door. "You're not leaving?" I shouted.

"Lord n-no," said Tom, who stuttered a little in moments of excess. "I-I'm just going home to p-pick up my telescope."

He set it up in the side yard. It was a warm August night; the Milky Way appeared to be breathing in and out. I made a mental note for the revision of my novel (an agent had it now, was sending it around.) "It's a g-grand night," said Tom. "I thought the g-girls might get a kick out of w-watching the stars." He winked.

One by one they sneaked out to peer through the lens: Lillian O., then Bob T.; Martha F., followed by Chuck L.

Three divorces came out of that evening, although I don't think we can take all the blame. The groundwork had been laid, I'm sure, long before; the paint fumes only let the beast escape out of the civilized psyche. At five a.m. I was awakened by a plaintive call from Janet L. Her husband hadn't come home yet. Spence and I were in bed; the last couple had reeled away at four-thirty.

"Oh dear," I said. "Maybe he had car trouble. Wait, though — " Outside I heard the murmur of voices, a car revving up, grinding softly away down the road. A second peeled off in the opposite direction.

"He was here, after all," I told Janet. "He'll be driving in your yard in a min. Goo-night."

The children woke me at nine o'clock. The house smelled of paint, my head ached. "Mom, come see!" said Lesley, pulling at my nightgown. "Out in the field. A star thing!"

"I know," I said. "I don't want to see it now." The Milky Way still shimmered in front of my eyes. I stumbled into the living room.

There it was, in pristine splendor. They'd painted everything — walls, ceiling, doors, floors, windows — even the window glass. Henry Swider was already at work, trying to scrape it off. "It must've been some night," he said.

"I wanted it white," I moaned, "but not everything white."

"It's not all white. Who won this game of tic-tac-toe?" he asked, scraping at a window pane.

"Oh no! On the window, too? Where did they get the red paint for that?"

He shrugged. "Well, don't worry about a thing," he said, patting my arm. "We'll fix it up. Old Henry's here."

A Dollar and
Two Beers an Hour

"SPENCE. SPENCE! HEY, WAKE UP! Charlie Willson's here. He says he's reporting for work."

" 'Z only two o'glock ina moring," my husband said, his nose squashing deeper into the pillow. "Go azleep. I juz gotto bed."

"It's six o'clock, not two," I said. "And he needs you to tell him what to do."

"Gee-zum," he moaned. He'd been outside mixing cement in the wheelbarrow by the light of an iron floorlamp — a beacon in the night to Route 30 truck drivers rumbling past the sleeping houses of Cornwall.

"Better run downa store and geta six-pack," he said, dragging himself out of bed.

"For lunch, you mean."

"For breakfast. Charlie takes a beer every hour. Sometimes two. Better make it three six-packs."

"Store doesn't open for two hours yet," I reminded him.

"Well, he'll prob'ly have some with him to start." He staggered out, buttoning his shirt. "Charlie? We'll start on the upstairs today. Charlie! Charlie?"

But Charlie was already on his way up to the shop loft. He'd remembered the spinning wheel. It was to go to the lake camp. The rest of the debris he'd already removed or stowed away in the shop attic. "Ready down there?" he shouted out the open top door. "Here she co-om-mes." And he lowered the split pieces of the spinning wheel into Spence's lethargic arms. Grinning, he squinted down at us through round steel spectacles, a robust septuagenarian in red suspenders and long white underwear that peeked out under the cuffs of his khaki workpants.

After two years of stalemate the shop was now shooting out in all directions. The room to the south was underway. The upstairs was about to become a display area; a foundation was being laid for a storage space in back. Somewhat frustrated by his duties as guardian of Ruth Wright's "geegaws," Charlie allowed himself to be slowly lured over to Spence's camp.

At first it was small jobs: mowing the lawn, or, when the vetch and sumac won out, repairing the mower. "I think it's pretty well broke," Charlie would say, eyeing the hunk of rusted steel. Or helping to plant a small vegetable garden. He never read the instructions on the backs of the envelopes: "Lord didn't have no seed catalogues," he'd say, heaving in the seed and then heaping the dirt generously over it. And the plants grew as cheerfully as if it had been the Lord's hand that sowed them there.

An affinity for the land was in his bones. Born in 1890 of old Vermont stock, Charlie was an outdoors man from the first. Motherless at the age of four, he went west to Nebraska with his father to work in the wheat fields there. His schooling was constantly interrupted; after grade four he called it quits. The books didn't teach him what he really wanted to know: where to find the biggest pike, or how far above the timber line the bear had his den. Bored with the flatlands, he returned at last to Vermont and found work on a farm. Saturday nights he would go dancing or celebrate a victory with his baseball team. An old photo shows him lying in uniform at the feet of his teammates, an easy smile on his broad, flushed face.

It was in the muddy gun positions of World War I that his outdoor education paid off. The men of his 302nd Field Artillery were toppling all around him, he said, cut down by the German shells and howitzers. Any minute it might be his turn. It was autumn 1918, and they were advancing on a dying enemy near St. Mihiel. But Charlie knew the fury of a wounded animal; even though the enemy was nearly defeated, he must still be cautious. His battery was all but wiped out. And then a thick mist crept up around. He couldn't see the hand in front of his face, he said; there were only the screaming shells and the cries of the wounded. "One step at a time" he made it through, on "cat feet." He owed his life, he said, to that fog.

After the war he would never attend a funeral; he'd seen too many dead men. He distrusted automobiles and he refused to speak on the telephone. Some inexplicable fear would come over him, a sense of entrapment. For a time he avoided people; lived alone in the Cornwall swamp on the bank of Otter Creek, near the cave where the legendary Ann Story hid her children from marauding Indians back in 1774. There, in a silence magnified by his damaged eardrums, he fished, trapped, and hunted, cutting and selling wood only when he needed money. He was happiest, he claimed, when the fog drifted up from the creek and cut him off from the rest of the world.

It was diminutive Rena Towle, a foot shorter than he, who lured him back into the world. The pair married, restored an old house that by all accounts "outbroke" the Broken House, and had two children. John, the younger, later bought the Boardman house next door to us and became the best of neighbors. Charlie plunged back into life, mastered a half dozen trades — electrician, plumber, farmer, carpenter, painter of steeples. He walked out on roofs and high wires where only birds dared to tread. The man with the cat feet, they called him.

A dollar an hour he charged back in 1945 when he first started to work for Ruth and Stanley Wright. A dollar an hour he charged two decades later. He worked for people, he said, not pay.

"But times have changed," Spence argued, "you have to consider inflation."

"I'm getting along in years," Charlie would say, shaking his craggy head. "Want to set my own pace."

When the fish decided to jump, or hunting season came along, Charlie was off, on his cat feet. He wouldn't take a penny of sick pay or overtime. He even deducted his beer breaks. At the end of the week he would frown over the notepad he carried with him in his shirt pocket and inform us of the precise amount owed him. It usually came out to something like seven dollars and twenty-six cents for an eight-hour day. If he found himself overpaid, he'd "owe" us an hour. What did he need money for, anyway? Taxes, a little food — beyond that he and his wife owed no one.

Rena was cut from the same cloth. A friend told me once that Rena had charged her $3.81 for a huge bundle of washing and ironing. What was the cent for? she wondered. And there was the time an envelope containing a five-dollar bill blew out of a basket of wash young Danny Wright took down to the Willson house. Rena found it the next spring when the snow thawed. Why was she getting all this money? she asked my mother-in-law, and tried to give it back.

To this day Rena, who babysat Spence when she was a high school student, is the only one allowed to patch his workpants, in a maze of handstitching that would cross younger eyes in seconds. Asked how much he owes her: "Oh, gimme a dollar," she'll say. "That's enough."

Where Henry preferred to work in silence, Charlie's work rhythm rose and fell on the telling of old tales (and the hourly beer). Once started, he was like a wind-up phonograph, spinning through from start to finish. Anyone with a question would have to shout it afterward. If he weren't already launched into a second tale, and if he chose to, for he wasn't above using his deafness to advantage, he'd give an answer. The stories were about the war, of course, or hunting: for instance, the 240-pound bear he shot up in Goshen, and dragged back single-handed through the underbrush.

And there were the John Alden stories. Unlike the *Mayflower* John, who couldn't speak for himself, Johnny Alden of Whiting, Vermont, had a lot to say. A bachelor and odd-job man who lived with his mother in Charlie's heyday, John was both hero and victim of the stories he inspired. There was the time his mother was after him about a mouse she'd seen sneaking around the parlor. She nagged at her son for three weeks straight. At last John marched out to the woodshed, loaded his shotgun "and pumped that friggin' mouse full of buckshot!"

Then there was the time his new Model T refused to start.

John tinkered with it for two or three hours, finally "blowed his stack," according to Charlie, "hied hisself over to the rail fence, picked up a ten-foot pole, and pounded the hood with all his might. 'Now ye'll go, damn ye!' he hollered at the automobile. And by gosh if he ain't bent the en-tire hood plumb down over the gawddamn engine!"

Charlie was upstairs in the shop, relating one of the more unsavory stories, when a pair of perfumed ladies came in to browse.

"Oh, is there an upstairs too?" one of them asked.

"There will be by the end of summer," I replied. "They're working on it now."

"Working?" she repeated as a rumble of laughter came from the loft, and then the sound of clinking bottles. She lifted a stockinged leg onto the bottom step. Clinging to the ancient ropes that served as bannister, she began to climb.

It was another John Alden story Charlie was relating. I'd heard it before. John's mother had sent him to the Whiting store to fetch groceries. His dog, a giant, black curbstone setter with mean yellow eyes, sat guard inside the automobile. The keys were still in the ignition. Sam would never move, John bragged to a couple of the boys who happened to be there in the store, " 'Not less I tell 'im to, and I ain't plannin' on it.' Wal, the boys bet John a five-dollar bill they'd get that doggone dog out of there. 'Haw haw,' John laughed, 'ye'll never do it.' And he ordered another five bucks' worth of beer."

"There's really nothing up there yet," I called up quickly to the woman.

"But I see a charming old basket," she said, craning her neck.

"It's my mother-in-law's," I assured her. "I mean, not for sale at all."

"Five bucks!" Charlie bellowed. "Johnny thought he'd got 'em this time. But he didn't. He come outa the store and by gum ain't no dog in that automobile! Just the boys, about to take off for a joy ride. 'Ye owe us five bucks, John,' they hollered at 'im."

The woman was at the top step now, her hand reaching out to touch the basket. I heard Spence's voice, shushing Charlie. But the storyteller prevailed:

" 'How'd ye get 'im outta there?' John wants to know. 'That dog don't move for nobody or nothin' on earth!' Then he seen the dog cringing over by a tree, his tail between his legs."

"Charlie!" Spence shouted. "I need your help over here with this beam."

" 'Hell, it was easy,' the boys told Johnny: 'We just opened up and pissed all over 'im. That damn dog jumped outa that automobile so fast you'da thought he had springs on!' "

The woman came down the steps just as fast, her hands scraping on the rope. "My, those steps are steep," she said, fanning herself. "Oh, my!"

The upstairs, it seemed, built itself on Charlie's stories. In a year or two we were a two-story shop, with a rear addition underway. Spence was always assured of a good carpenter. If Charlie was off hunting bear or spading up Ruth Wright's garden at the lake, Henry was there. If Henry was out fishing or on a surveying job, Charlie was usually with us, suspenders hoisted up over the long underwear he wore year-round. Then one Friday in July when they both happened to be gone, a third carpenter came along.

Spence was struggling under a six-foot beam with only a complaining Gary on the other end when a young woman with a mane of shiny red hair swung into the shop. Her name was Caroline Fairless, and she took us by surprise with her request. Her brother Ben had been a student of ours at Proctor Academy. Her grandfather, we knew, had been chairman of the board at U.S. Steel. She wanted to buy some land to build a house on — with her own hands. "I'm here to learn how," she said.

Returning the next day with a string of perch for our freezer, our two regular carpenters were startled to see a tall, husky redhead in jeans bending over what resembled, more or less, the legs of a sawhorse. It was her first assignment. Out of every three blows of the hammer, only one hit the nail.

"Spen-sah, you're not serious now. You're not going to hire that girl!" said Henry.

Charlie tucked a wad of Redman tobacco inside his cheek, and chuckling softly to himself, shuffled back upstairs.

Caroline bent fiercely to her task. By the end of the day she had three of the four legs on the sawhorse. The freckles stood out damply on her face.

"A see-sawhorse," Henry said. "I mean, what does she think she's doing, Spen-sah? She ought to be home clipping her coupons."

Monday morning Caroline arrived at eight a.m., a nail apron over her jeans, a smug look on her face. The men were already at work. Henry glanced up and sighed as she strode over to her sawhorse. A minute later he looked again. Caroline's hammer was rising and falling in a steady rhythm, driving the nails home. In twenty minutes the sawhorse was completed. She gave it a little wiggle to show how sturdy it was and smiled at the men.

"I'm seeing things," said Henry.

Charlie stopped chewing.

She'd practiced all day Sunday, she told them, filling up an old apple log with three kegs of nails. "So what's next?" she asked Spence.

After that the men took her seriously. Henry even gave her tips and books on carpentry. When she purchased a piece of land up in New Haven, he surveyed it, and took a teacher's pride in her progress on the new house. "Not bad," he'd say, "for a female."

As for Charlie, he accepted Caroline's presence the way an old dog will accept a neighborly duck: ignoring the thing with feathers for a while, finally accepting the presence as inevitable. "Try it this way," he'd say. When she'd done the task correctly he'd give a grunt of approval, and taking advantage of a fresh ear, launch into a tale of old John Alden, or the foggy assault on the Huns of World War I.

It was the St. Mihiel fog that almost did him in one morning. He was sawing lumber, heaving the boards one by one up to Spence, who was braced on the top rung of a stepladder. Artillery-man Charlie was slogging up the road, the shells shrieking about him "when this tree-menjous fog come rolling in," he told Caroline. "A reg'lar pea soup — you was in it head to toe. And a good thing, with the Huns up ahead, just waiting."

"Another board, Charlie," Spence yelled. "Up here."

"Lost our direction, too. Ever stuck your head in a bowl of pea soup? Try to figure north from south?"

Caroline hadn't. She shook her head. Charlie tossed the board up to Spence, went on with his story.

The board fell short and wide, as if it, too, had lost direction. Spence made a grab, but missed. Caroline ran for it, but too late. The board swung back and whacked Charlie on the nose, shattering his glasses. For a moment he stood there, as if struck by a random shell. Blood spurted from his nostrils, red as the suspenders that held up his baggy pants.

In seconds Caroline had us mobilized: Spence, Henry —myself in from the shop. She sat Charlie on the sawhorse she'd built, barked out orders like an army nurse: "Hot water. Iodine. Clean gauze. Aspirin."

"Beer!" yelped Charlie.

"You're okay, Charlie," Caroline said. "It might have hit you in the head. You were lucky it was just your nose. The fog saved you again."

Charlie nodded. Fifteen minutes later he was back on the job, his face swathed in bandages, hazel eyes squinting through a pair of Spence's reading glasses. He concentrated on his work, all stories abandoned for the day. The broken glasses scrunched in his pocket, sealed up in a Cornwall Crafts envelope. We insisted on buying him a new pair. Just as vehemently he declined. "My own fault," he maintained. "Rena says I tell too many stories. Maybe I do."

"Don't stop telling them, Charlie," Caroline urged. A story-teller herself, she later wrote Hambone, an award-winning children's book. Even then, she was still living alone in the "plumbless" house she'd built to hold the world at bay, like Charlie in his post-war cabin on Otter Creek. A woman growing up in the sixties, she'd faced her own wars, in her own way.

Charlie took Caroline's advice: the stories went on. New glasses seemed to bring new energy — or remind him of his mortality. He came to work one day in his "dancing shoes." Of prewar vintage, they were handcrafted, black and high-buckled. "Bout time I got the wear out of 'em," he said. "They don't make 'em like this today." And he did a little shuffle to show how they used to do it in the Saturday night "kitchen hops" when he was a young blade, with girls' voices exploding in his ears instead of shells.

"Now there's a real Vermonter. Get a picture of him!" a customer urged her husband as Charlie passed through the shop in his black shoes. In one hand was a hammer, in the other a six-pack of beer. It was the last weekend in June, and he was trying to complete the upstairs.

The customer was trying to match up a pair of stoneware mugs from the selection by a local potter. "That's the beauty of them," I tried to explain. "I mean, the irregularity. No two are alike."

"Oh dear," she said after Charlie disappeared upstairs. The lines fell into parentheses around her mouth. "Couldn't he make another to match this one? It's so perfectly round."

"I don't think I can get him to do that," I said.

"Well, I don't want just one," she said, and put the mugs back. "Bob!" she hollered at her husband, who was now outdoors photographing the shop so thoroughly that I wondered if he was with the Mafia, or the IRS. He trotted in, a huge camera hanging about his neck. "So what's goin' on in here?" he said.

I turned away, afraid he might ask to see my shop "books" — loosely kept records, to say the least, Spence and I being prime examples of the "left hand disconnected from the right." But I heard the pair whispering, and a moment later, stomping up the steps. "Hi, there," the man said when he reached the top. The front half was full of furniture and woodenware; Charlie would be working in the unfinished half.

There was an answering grunt, and then the whack of a hammer. Although customers often greeted him, they usually left him alone when they saw he was preoccupied. I was wary, though, of this pair with a camera. I tiptoed up to the stair landing; some prints on the wall needed straightening.

"Wouldja mind standin' over here in the light?" the man asked him. "I wanna get a pitcher."

There was no reply from Charlie. The hammering went on.

"Take him where he is, Bob," said the woman. "Get him working."

"Nice shoes ya got there," Bob said. "My grandfather had a pair jus' like 'em."

Another grunt, then even more feverish hammering.

"If ya ever wanna sell 'em," said Bob, "I got a kid collects old stuff like 'at."

Bob was focusing, ready to shoot, when his wife screamed. I dashed up. A bird had flown in through the open loft door. It was a swallow; I'd seen her before. I'd close the door now and then to discourage her, but she'd managed to start a nest up in one of the rafters. This time it looked as though she'd chosen a new nest site on the captain's chair below, where the woman was sitting. The swallow was circling the woman's head, round and round, while the latter gave out an unremitting series of shrieks.

"What is it — a hawk? Get it away from me, Bob. Bob! Do something, Bob, for God's sake!"

"It's not a hawk," Bob said. "It's jus' a tiny bird. A sparrow or somepin'." And he backed into a corner and snapped his wife's picture.

"If you'll get up out of there," Charlie told the woman, "she'll leave you be. You're settin' on her nest." He grinned down at her, hands on his hips.

"How can I get up?" she wailed. "It's attacking me! Do something. Don't just stand there!"

Charlie raised his eyebrows. I grabbed her arm. Still wailing, she allowed me to pull her over to the sanctuary of the stairwell. The swallow snatched up a bit of straw from her squashed nest and zoomed off. Part of the nest was still stuck to the back of the woman's skirt. I shut the loft door on Bob's camera, where he was taking pictures of the "sparrow's" flight.

Charlie was chuckling to himself as the woman minced down the steps. "Bob!" she screeched as she reached the bottom. Bob took a quick snap of Charlie and followed.

"Well, you weren't any help!" we heard her accuse.

"Come on, Rose," he said. "You're always makin' mountains outa mouseholes."

"Neither was he," she said. "That old Vermonter. He just stood there and laughed."

"So?" he said. "He's a character, 'at's all. There's a lotta characters in this state. You read about 'em all the time."

"Wall, they'll all be gone soon, back to Noo York," Charlie said, just a little louder than he needed to, and winking at me, padded back to work in his black buckled shoes.

Several years after that he developed cancer of the lung. Bookseller Dike Blair and his wife, whose clean shirts were the product of Rena's labors, drove him up, with Rena, to the Burlington Medical Center for radiation treatments. One day he rebelled. "Enough," he told the doctors. "It's the treatment that's killing me."

He survived a few months longer, then died at home, aged eighty-four, in a bed Rena set up in the dining room. Eighty-four was old enough, he'd said. Spence and I went down to the house to pay our last respects where he lay in an open coffin amid a gathering of family and friends: dressed up the way we seldom saw him in life —but in his dancing shoes. The soles, I noticed, looked worn.

"Better drive slowly. It's a foggy night," I said to Spence on our way home to the Broken House.

"Good," he said. "Old Charlie's safe now."

A Crock to Carry Mother In

BY THE EARLY SEVENTIES Aunt Evelyn was having attacks of "old bones," she said, and called up to excuse herself from the fall shopkeeping.

We were living in the Broken House year-round by then: I'd left teaching to run the shop, and write. At least I managed to scribble three to four hours each morning, with the help of a succession of summer "shop persons." The latter ranged through the years from tiny Nikki, who had to stand on tiptoe to see over the counter, to over-six-foot Christina, who startled customers by looming up suddenly with a joyful greeting. (She later became a minister for the United Church of Christ.)

"What will I tell the customers if you don't come?" I asked Evelyn.

"Tell them I drowned in my cataracts."

"So you admit you have cataracts! Promise you'll go right to an ophthalmologist and tell him your problem."

"Op-yours," she replied. "That's what I'll tell him."

She ended the conversation with a request for another hobby horse. "I think I can sell 'em down here."

"Hmm," I said, gazing at the ceiling. And thus began what was to metamorphose into a hobby horse empire.

Local craftsman Jack Brown was willing to turn them out in quantity. A bright and personable young Vermonter, Jack seemed the right sire for "Timothy." Besides, Charlie Willson had once worked for Jack, and pronounced him a "good fellow." Brown Novelty Company, established in 1936 by Jack's father and uncle on the site of an 1827 sash and door plant, made wooden parts for a number of items, including 150,000 toy pianos. Charlie worked there when the machinery was run by a horizontal water wheel. The shaft the wheel turned is still in use for grinding out the Cornwall Horse, as the latter came to be called.

A handsome, sturdy horse of Vermont pine and maple with an antique pine finish, Timothy would also come "knock-down," complete with assembly instructions. Although at first most of our wholesale accounts were small shops with names like Dandy Lion, Kiddie Kloset, Wood N'Hand, and Gillie Wrinkles, we soon established larger ones, such as Jenifer House in Massachusetts. The owner, Karl Lipsky, was a friend of our carpenter lady, Caroline Fairless, who offered to drive down the wooden beasts. "She will be well received," Lipsky wrote back. "She will have fresh flowers on her night table, hand-squeezed orange juice in the morning, and farm eggs blushed in bubbling butter. And your Cornwall horse will be featured on the back cover of *Yankee*."

He kept his promise on all accounts.

Our ultimate account, we hoped, was to be the famous F.A.O. Schwarz in the heart of New York City. We drove to the Big Apple one spring day, hauling Timothy down Fifth Avenue and up to the head buyer's office:

"Too plain," said Mr. Tadhofer. "Give him a saddle — cloth or leather — something jazzy. And we'll send along a purchase order. You bet."

We were a bit wary. Several shops had offered plans for "improvements" on Timothy. A local woodcarver tried to persuade us to let him sculpt a new head; he whipped out a drawing of a great, foaming Eohippus with a snarly upturned lip and huge pointed teeth. "You need passion, drive, in this horse," he said.

"Sorry, but uh, it's not quite what we have in mind for our clientele," we told him.

Since Brown's was producing the horse in quantity, even the

tiniest alteration meant new patterns, increased labor, in short —
more money. As it was, we only netted three dollars a horse after
we paid Jack. F.A.O. Schwarz, though, meant volume. We had fifty
red quilted saddles made up by a local seamstress and sent along a
sample to Mr. Tadhofer. Three months later we received a reply:
"This is to advise you that we are returning the sample under
separate cover. Mr. Tadhofer has left our employ. As his replacement I must tell you that the saddle detracts from the horse. If you
are willing to design a new tail, however, we will give the item our
careful consideration. Roy Fox."

The three months preceding Christmas were always frenetic.
Jack Brown and his merry men couldn't keep up with the orders;
several Christmas Eves we were out until midnight delivering
horses still sticky with fresh stain. Shops phoned in at all hours of
the day demanding them, citing problems: a broken tail, an
unglued eye. "Our problem," one customer wrote, "is that the kit
contained six (6) legs instead of four (4) legs, and only two (2) cross
braces. My two (2)-legged son is now riding a legless (0) horse."

The merry-go-round spun on for nine years. Although we
never caught the brass ring — Schwarz vetoed the new tail — the
experience was at once fun and frustrating, sad and wonderful.
Consider the letters from one small shop in New Hampshire:

Old Village Barn, June 12, 1974

Dear Mrs. Wright: I placed a new horse on the floor
today and one of the eyes popped out. My wife and I
searched on our knees — in vain. The little girl who was to
have it wept. So I took an eye out of another head and they
went away happy. Thanks for your kind attention.
Richard L.

June 26, 1974: Thank you for sending the horse head.
My granddaughter, after a long search, came up with the
missing eye. If you have some special glue you might send
it over and I will insert the eye in the head. We hope the
tourists won't lose their enthusiasm for buying, with
escalating food prices and diminishing gas. So would you
please send the rest of the horse to go with the new head?

Mrs. L., alas, is in the hospital with a stroke and my household duties have doubled, not to mention the shop. R.L.

9/3/74: My son-in-law has been helping me as some of the screw holes drilled in the head do not match those in the seat. I am terribly worried as I just shipped one a 1000 miles to a lady who might not be at all mechanical. I will phone her and explain how to adjust the holes just in case. We shall continue to feature handsome Timothy right thru the foliage season. You might use heavier twine to tie the boxes together for UPS. Mrs. L. is home now, thank you. R.L.

5/12/75: Check enclosed to hold six horses at the usual $18.90 each. Progress has come slowly to Mrs. L. No improvement on the right arm or hand. Had a slight setback this week, a cold set in and then she slipped and banged her ankle, causing swelling in her good left foot. She's so fond of Timothy. Trust you folks are well and that spring has finally come to your area — something Mrs. L. likes very much. Don't ship the horses yet. Dick L.

8/26/75: The writer has very carefully wrapped each damaged piece in several thicknesses of newspaper with lots of padding inside the package. You might ask your man to place the screws entirely away from the seat and head. Please do not make us a "special case" — that was not our intention at all. What we are most interested in is to make an imprint on every customer that this is the BLUE RIBBON OF ROCKING HORSES and handmade in Vermont by careful craftsmen. Nothing pleases me more than to demonstrate to the children and their grandmothers the value of this fine horse. You might ask your man about the idea of drilling the head hole a half inch higher. Hope you are well. Dick L.

10/7/75: A sorry shipment today. Oh don't infer any blame on your part. This time UPS did us in. When he appeared he was dragging three pretty rough-looking cartons. He said something had tipped over in the truck and they got wet. UPS doesn't carry perishables, so how could they get wet? I went right to work taking apart the water-soaked boxes — I assume it was water — and then re-wrapped the cartons, Mrs. L. spurring me on from her chair. Will water hurt the finish? Again please note this is not your fault. Being alone running the shop I'll have to wait until I can get some spare time to finish the rewrapping. Yours, Dick.

7/12/76: PLEASE SHIP THE SIX ROCKING HORSES WE ENGAGED LAST MAY. Remember the heavy binder twine to tie boxes. I have been late opening this season because of the death of my dear Mary. The loss of a gallant lady who stood by me for over forty-six years comes hard. We had our reservations to fly back from our vacation home in Arizona when she suffered another massive stroke. She passed away last month. I flew back alone four days later. Will let you know when we will need more horses. I wonder how I'm going to bear up this season. Dick.

8/18/76: Two legs in recent shipment have scratches, kindly send along replacements. This horse is an outstanding piece of work and we tell our customers so. It is a little rough battling the duties of the shop alone but I'm making out OK. Will be happy when the black flies leave, trust you folks are not bothered with them. Again many thanks for your good service and hope that you and your husband will find your way here one day for a visit. You forgot to put the Timothy flyers in your last shipment. Yours, Dick.

8/9/77: A problem with Mrs. F's Kindergarten in Portland. The tail hole was ¼ out of proportion she said and the tail was broken. I'd be willing to bet she botched up the job trying to fix the hole, and split the tail herself. Well, anyway. We know you must be busy and happy with your shop. Please send along a replacement tail or better yet bring it. Dick.

6/18/79: Thank you for returning the call relative to the lost horse that was to go to our customer's granddaughter in Texas. The letter you mentioned about "burn-out" and transferring the wholesale end of the horse business to Jack Brown did not arrive this morning (hence my letter) but we presume it will turn up tomorrow. The writer was very sorry to hear it. He would like to thank you for your many kindnesses, and for the fine product you have rendered to us over the years. We shall miss that contact very much. We shall continue to promote this wonderful horse season after season as long as the writer can operate the Old Country Barn. Yours very truly, Dick.

P.S. Please tell Mr. Brown he can expect in the mail a plan for a slight alteration to the "splitting" tail.

Even though we were again selling horses retail only, Christmas Eve invariably found one family member out delivering, another in the shop (covering me while I warbled in the Cornwall church choir) to receive the husbands/fathers/lovers come to pick up lamps or rocking chairs or coffee tables. Men, we discovered, accounted for ninety percent of the last-minute holiday shoppers.

"What can I get for a woman who has everything?" a middle-aged man asked one December 24.

"Your mother?" I asked.

"Wife. It's a second marriage. A second set of presents came with it."

"Oh. I see. Well —." I led him about the shop. "A new lamp? A set of mugs? They're always breaking, you know. How about this hand-thrown vase? You could put flowers in it. Or pewter?"

"Sold," he said.

"Which? The vase? the pewter?"

"Whatever you think she'd like best."

And so we were back on square one. Invariably the mats or vase or pewter I chose would reappear for a post-Christmas exchange: "He knew I wanted that cranberry lamp upstairs," she'd say. "Did I have to hit him over the head with it?"

The holidays over, I could concentrate on my writing. The shop was slow in winter; we couldn't afford to hire anyone.

Besides, no one in her right mind would work in the bone-cold barn. For several years after we opened year-round we had no heat at all. "The energy crunch, you know," was the excuse for a year or two, until oil became more plentiful, and then it was: "Sorry. Heat's off today."

"You poor thing," the customer would say. "And they expect you to work in this deep-freeze?"

"May I quote you to my husband?" I'd say. And watch while she fairly galloped about the shop to keep the cold from boring into her bones.

"Well, I don't really need anything today. I'll try to come back next weekend," she'd say, and dash out into the relative warmth of the winter sun.

"Try next spring," I'd murmur, and clomp back to the type-writer in my husband's Christmas gift: a pair of outsized fur-lined Eskimo boots that turned my feet to fiery furnaces inside the wood-heated house.

It was news of the shop, not my fiction, that Spencer demanded when he came home from work. He was in real estate now, selling land and old houses. He'd been somehow born for the job.

"If you miss the shop so much," I said, "you can take over, starting tomorrow."

"It's too big now," he argued. "I wouldn't know how."

This was true, I realized. With the help of Peter Hincks's loan, he and Henry Swider had built a barn at the budding "tree farm," a half mile away on Cider Mill Road, to contain the overflow of shop "things." In icy weather, when the ten-year-old van we'd bought refused to climb the hill, we'd carry a chest or table down the slope between us: "Watch out for that baby tree!" Spence would holler: "Loogout! There's another!" "I don't care!" I'd yell back like our friend Virginia Graham, as I bore blindly bottomward.

"So what went on today in the shop?" he'd repeat, pouring himself a glass of wine and sighing into a chair.

"Well — " I'd say, and echo his sigh.

9/7/71: Today I stood two hours outside the barn while Mr. Z. checked every knothole in eighteen Viking chairs. One sunburn later he asked: "If you were my wife, which two would you choose?" Somehow, I'd heard that song before. "Well —," I hemmed. "Never mind," he said, "I don't dare choose without her." And left me with eighteen chairs, like the lady who'd put the wrong date on her party invitations.

11/9/71: "Dear Mrs. Wright: I was sorry to miss you yesterday when you and your husband drove the furniture down here to Long Island. Anyway, I am writing to let you know that the table and hutch you delivered are the wrong ones."

4/15/72: Sole customer today: a woodchuck — admiring the placemats when I walked in. "He bought two blue ones," I told Spence. "He must be expecting company," said S.

5/5/72: "Give a holler now if you have any questions!" I sang out as usual when the couple walked in. "Only question I have is, can I afford it?" the man hollered back.

6/10/72: "Weatherman says clouds'll blow over, no rain," said Yankee Pinecraft over in New Hampshire as Don and I tied the unfinished trestle table to the top of the station wagon. Halfway to Vermont came the deluge: Don hanging out the window to clutch one side of a piece of plastic, myself the other. Every ten minutes a skidding stop to sponge off the table. "So it'll be one big rain spot. Who's going to say anything?" said Don. "It's for the Fullers," I said. "Virginia Graham will have something to say." "Oh," he said.

7/9/72: "Dear Driver: After your St. Johnsbury truck backed into our van this morning we discovered it had banged in our left door and demolished the tire. Can we work something out?"

8/2/72: Lady trying to choose between two ceramic owls, both from the same mold: "Which expression do you like best?"

10/11/73: Santa Claus walked into the shop — from Santa's Land, over in New York. Complete with red suit, bells, and beard. He bought a gun cabinet.

11/2/73: "Dear Folks: Sorry about the warping on the Taggert hutch. All we can say is that we stand behind our work, and that this sometimes happens, as wood is more unpredictable than woman. Yrs, Yankee Pinecraft Co."

"That letter has a familiar ring," I said to Spence.

11/6/73: "Dear M/M Taggert: How are you coming on getting the two warped doors off the hutch? We will rush them right over to the plant when they arrive, and pay shipping as well. We understand your reason for holding off payment — although the hutch was on sale. N.W."

12/5/73: "Remember me, Mrs. Wright? The lady who fell in love with your shop? Well the new table arrived today, and looks fine. I hated losing my old round table, for my late husband and I shared many happy (and some unhappy) memories around it. But this apartment dining room is too small for that table. I'll try to get used to yours. L.P."

1/9/74: "Dear M/M Taggert: I was truly sorry to hear about illness in the family, and your financial problems. We can't solve the warped door problem, however, until we get the doors. Please help."

2/20/74: A group of Japanese today: picking up everything, exclaiming in Japanese. In the end, in perfect English (as they walked out): "Thank you please for your lovely exhibition."

"You should have passed the cup," said Spence.

3/9/74: "Dear M/M Taggert: We shipped a new door by UPS today. I promise you it is perfectly straight."

4/7/74: "The Cornwall horse arrived in perfect condition. Muffin cried when she saw it. A picture enclosed of Muffin in her party dress. Gratefully, Muffin's Gram and Grampy."

4/7/74: "Dear M/M Taggert: According to our builders, the same finish is applied to all pieces — we can't see how the new door could be that much darker. Please return both old and new doors so we can see the difference. If it is indeed major, we will build a new one."

7/1/74: Our daughter Cathy's shop tale: the cat,

Carmen, one-upped a young man today after the fellow stepped on the beast, and despite the howls, stood there, heel pressed solidly on the hapless tail. When at last he lifted his foot, Carmen gave the fellow a sharp right to the calf and took off. Thereby hangs a tail.

8/19/74: "Dear M/M Taggert: We have now sent along three new doors. Please pick the closest match and return the others — hopefully along with your check. This experience has inspired us to institute a no return policy on sale pieces."

10/3/74: "Dear Cornwall Crafts family: I've forgotten your name. I think of Wright — or was that your delightful aunt's name? Anyway, I had two Australian guests who fell in love with the rocking chair my friend Amy and I bought last summer. Would it be too much trouble to ship one to Sydney, Australia? Rose Fish."

1/4/75: Cathy told Maggie S.'s father on the phone about the six dollars Maggie has owed us for seven months. Five minutes later M. comes racing up the icy shop walk, the money clutched in her fist, trips over the duck, and dives at the glass door — a clean break.

For us no break at all — the new pane cost six dollars.

3/12/75: "Sydney, Australia: The rocker arrived safely. Hope it wasn't any trouble to send. Amy and I are here, too! A travelogue enclosed of our adventures, along with a kangeroo for Cathy and a pet rock for yourself. Rose Fish."

7/7/75: E.K. Rokes, my New Hampshire "birdhouse" man, was bitten by a woman's Pekingese. I administered first aid while she wrung her hands and apologized. As she swept the beastie up in her arms, its tail knocked over a glass bird feeder. "Here, doggie, here's some feed for you," growled Rokes, holding out the bits of glass.

9/3/75: Fall bicycle tour (Bronx to Quebec) dropped by (literally). Net results: Ten plastic bottles filled with water, pump exhausted after ten flushes, band-aids used up on finger cut after handlebars fell off, and dog lost her voice barking. Spence drove the broken bicycle to town in the van for repairs.

10/13/75: "Gotta wastebasket?" asked a woman. Wherein she deposited five apple cores and a loaded diaper.

2/2/76: "New South Wales, Australia: I want to do a little refurbishing in a house we're renting (my friend unwell). Recall those Turco paints. A yellow, I think — the second or third yellow down on your chart? (or gold?) Please send two quarts. Hope you know the one I mean. Rose Fish."

4/22/76: Competition in the shop today: Donald trying to sell Bicycle Bodi-Bouncer couple a table: ended up Don's buying a Bodi-Bouncer. "With his money, dammit!" said Spence.

2/30/77: "New South Wales, Australia. Thank you for the paint. I won't be needing it now, I'm coming home. My friend, the blue-eyed Amy, died in the spring. It's hard not to be one of a pair any more. May I exchange the paint for some of those lemon placemats? Rose Fish."

5/15/77: Allegheny Airlines Air Freight Arrival notice. Guadalajara, Mexico, to Burlington, Vermont. Collect: $112.60. "For ninety-eight dollars' worth of brandy glasses," I reminded Spence, who picked them out on our trip to old Mexico.

7/29/77: "Black River Workshop, Springfield, Vermont. Dear Good People: We received the six lovely 2' x 3' rag rugs made by your retarded clients. The bill puzzled us, however. $829.80? Could this be another fabrication of your clients?"

8/5/77: Sloan Wilson and his wife dropped in today. Catharine waiting on them when I arrived. S. a genial man in country clothes, peering at a lamp. "Mr. Wilson wrote *The Man in the Gray Flannel Suit,*" I explained to Catharine. Wilson nodding modestly. C. unimpressed: "My mother wrote *The Losing,*" she informed him. "About this lamp —," said Wilson.

3/13/78: Two myopic ladies gurgling over our new

cat, Catcher. Whereupon he flung a live chipmunk at their feet.

10/14/78: "Dear Cornwall Crafters: I couldn't sleep worrying about the travelers' checks I forgot to sign. Most places they watch me do it. A personal check enclosed for six of the brown Bennington mugs." The check was unsigned.

3/22/79: My writer friend June Noble and I drive to New Hampshire and back with van cram-full of furniture. Rain beginning to freeze on Bread Loaf Mountain. *June:* (as we slide slowly toward the precipice) Whoo-hoo! This old van can do anything, can't it? *Me:* Except stop. We just lost our brakes.

9/9/79: "A sincere thanks for returning my ring that fell through the crack in your floor boards. I'm impressed with your caring. Hope it wasn't too much of a job to take them up. Ann L."

5/11/79: Two letters received today: one to The Cornwall Horse, Vermont, 05753; the other to "the dark-haired, blue-eyed lady whose father makes cider." I delivered it next door to Jane Collier and hired her on a permanent basis. Inside the envelope was a fifty-dollar order.

9/9/79: The Cleven family dropped in today from Long Island with new pix of their grandchildren. Bought two Smead apple boards and one whale for new brides in their town. They claim only one cutting board split in twenty-two years of doing this, but no split marriages. "A whale of a record," said Spence.

1/2/80: To Lebo Lamp Co: "Thank you for the suggestion of sandpaper and rubbing alcohol to remove the glue from the lamp. The alcohol removed a bit of the glue and the sandpaper a lot of the glaze. We'll keep trying. Jane Collier."

2/2/80: "Attention, Jane Collier. Thank you for working with the glue problem on the lamp, there are not too many people that would even try to help by working with our company on manufacturing problems. Sincerely,

Michael, for Lebo Lamps. P.S. I am five-foot-nine and have red hair."

4/4/80: A local farmer this afternoon, wanting a two-gallon crock. "I gotta have a cover with it," he insisted, twisting his cap in his hands.

"I'm sorry," I told him, "but I can't get covers any more. Reynolds wrap is really all you need to cover pickles or whatever. Or maybe a plate on top?"

He stood there, turning his red cap. "It's not for pickles," he said.

"Well, meat then. Pork? We sell crocks for all kinds of things."

"Not for what I have in mind."

"What is it you have in mind?" I asked.

He swung back his head until he was looking down on me with heavy-lidded eyes. Then, flushing the color of his cap, said: "Well, goddammit — it's — well — it's for Mother. To bury her in!" And dashed out.

A minute later he was back in. "You wouldn't believe what they charge for urns," he said, "those undertakers. Hell, I'll take the crock anyway. How much, you say? Eight seventy-five? Here, keep the change." Peeling off nine new one-dollar bills, he slapped them down on the counter, stuck his cap back on his head, and strode out, the crock cradled under one arm. "Mother never approved of foolish spending!" he hollered back from his pickup.

"Here. You'll need a little of this," said Spence, handing me a tall glass of homemade wine.

"And you'll need a crock to carry me in," I said.

THE FAMILY

Change is the only permanence . . .

Horace, 1st century B.C.

A Delicate Balance

BACK IN 1963, the summer came on green and promising. With Henry's help we were building an addition on the shop, designed by Doc Collier next door, that would make us a two-room emporium. Indoors, by this time, we had a kitchen sink with running water and a drain that would suck the soiled water into a rusted pipe and out of sight through a dark hole in the floor. We had two indoor toilets — the second one upstairs in a converted closet with a faded red drape for a door. In this way we avoided the parade of little feet down the steps in the "wee" hours of the night, and the dreaded crash of the trap door that hung above the stairwell, propped open by two bookcases. To this day there is a broken board where the door came down on Gary one night as he stumbled downstairs unbuttoning his flap. The door gave way; he and it hung in balance a moment, then just as it swung down he crouched on the step, letting his shoulders bear the brunt.

By a downstroke of fate in the form of split lightning, the footsteps multiplied that summer, wearing away the varnish I'd laid on the old steps, and we had to install a gate at the top of the stairs to keep the little ones from tumbling.

The tragedy occurred one hot night in early July. We'd left the lake camp to make way for the arrival of the Charles Wright family, due in the next night, after Chuck's quick business trip to Rochester, New York. I was on the verge of my third summer at the French School. With our fourth child going on two, I would ride full-tilt into the windmill of French literature. We settled into the Broken House with our brood: Gary, a lean and hungry eleven-year-old with a diabolic imagination; Lesley, nine, with a Shirley Temple face that flashed sharp as a diamond when her will was thwarted; brick-haired Donald, a gentle, rawboned lad with a stubborn streak; and baby Catharine, a boop-cheeked cherub already focusing her eyes on the stairwell, and escape. At her age Donald had dropped through another trap door in the bedroom into the pantry below, where he landed, stunned, in a basket of potatoes. We were taking no chances with the youngest. We boarded up all floor openings except the trap door over the stairs, and lined up the older three to warn the grim consequences of leaving the stairwell gate unlocked.

On the night of the downward plunge the thermometer had soared to a giddy ninety degrees. We were lolling about in various stages of undress when the phone rang: it was Willie Galvin (hero-victim of the outhouse/electric fence incident) calling from Rochester, New York. His voice was high and thin. A Mohawk Airlines plane had climbed five hundred feet into an electric night and spun, crashing, to the ground. The pilot and seven others were killed on impact. The survivors, most of them IBM personnel, were rushed to the hospital. Thirty-six-year-old Chuck, Willie confirmed, had been on that flight. "Your brother's alive," Willie gasped over the phone, "but badly hurt."

"But he'll be here tomorrow," Mother W. protested when we called with the news. "I just had a letter from him!"

Chuck's wife, Barbara, had already heard when we telephoned their home in Wappingers Falls, New York. A former nurse, she was shaken but in control. "We're coming for the kids," we told her.

They were ready when Spence arrived. Mark, a solemn tow-headed lad, was concerned for his father, but anxious to help Uncle Spencer "take down one of those old barns." Sandy, a tall, blonde nine-year-old, ready for adventure, was tugging on the sleeve of her brother, Jimmy, a handsome, stoic child with a slight lisp. "I'm thtaying here, Uncle Thpencer," he announced, his legs spread wide on the carpet, his eyes round as moons, "my motherth bringing my father back — thoon!"

The child was enticed into the car with the promise of a swim in the lake and a quick return, and the trio borne off to Vermont, where they arrived at midnight, bewildered and subdued after a disciplinary "line-up" outside a Salem, New York, diner. They'd begun to wax hysterical, according to their weary uncle, fighting and crying in the back seat. At the Broken House we fed them milk and cookies and put them to bed, matching each with the cousin nearest in age. Our children received them in awe, like wounded warriors returning from a children's crusade. On the way upstairs Mark whispered to Lesley, "I think my dad has a broken neck," and while he lifted his tremulous chin, Lesley burst into tears.

At breakfast the next day we deployed our forces: The boys would make their room in the hut. Now a one-room structure behind our house, the hut was roofed but the sides were partly open to the weather. The older girls would share a double bed, with the promise of a hut-swap once a week. The roomy middle hall would make a nest for Jimmy and Donald, the tiny north room a berth for toddler Cathy. That left our unfinished bedroom, and a little garret off that where I sat hunched each night with my French assignments. When these were completed there was my new novel (my first was not to be published for another nine years). In late June my agent had encouraged the first fifty pages. By summer's end, all I had to show were fifty-one.

A hive of children, we discovered, attracts several times its number. Days before our arrival from New Hampshire for summer vacation, the tidings would fan out through the neighborhood: "the Wrights are coming!" and out we'd tumble, to be greeted by nine or ten pairs of eyes gleaming through the bushes. With seven children, the eyes (and stomachs) multiplied, and we were soon consuming three gallons of milk a day. In desperation my husband invented kickapoo juice, a mixture of iced tea and lemonade. Within days the neighborhood mothers were on the phone for the recipe — their offspring refusing to drink milk.

The post-breakfast Council of War became a daily affair, a

time to plan the day for the Cornwall Seven. It began with bed making. For our crew this meant sweeping the spread up over a rumple of sheets and blankets; the cousins tucked and smoothed, reflecting the training of a nurse-mother. Breakfast was a self-help meal: each child was assigned an initialed cup and plate that were whisked through the water at meal's end. Lunch was slapped together by the girls: twenty-five bologna sandwiches to be eaten by the kids, Henry Swider, the visitors on hand, and deaf old Charlie Willson, who was helping off and on that summer with the projected shop addition. He would put at least three bologna sandwiches and four beers under his red suspenders without losing a beat in the latest "old times" story he was telling.

To save housekeeping, meals were served outdoors on the patio, a stretch of green weeds behind the shop. Dinners, my job, were platters of gooey spaghetti or heaps of hamburgers, with contributions of Spanish rice or beef stew shipped up from the lake in vats by grandmother. Now and then we'd alter the menu with a bowl of pea soup, concocted by Spencer. He made up five gallons at a time in a steaming cauldron, which he then poured into an old chamberpot. At the sight of it the cousins turned as pea green as the contents. There was a post-pea-soup lineup in the house for the girls, and a rush into the bushes for the boys, who were allowed inside only for heavy-duty stuff.

The boy cousins never got to take down an old barn, but under the hammer of Uncle Spencer they were allowed to denail several old boards a day. With the help of the young Wood brothers from a nearby farm, the crew was an anvil chorus, hunched over the boards with glazed eyes, yanking and hammering to get out the rusty nails. Spence hovered over the raggedy crew like a Fagin over his gang of pickpockets, while Henry watched with amusement, yelling: "Come on Gary, come on Mark. Lasso those nails — don't let 'em get away!"

In the afternoon boys and girls were transferred up to the lot, a fifteen-acre hillside left over from the sale of the medical college property. The place crawled with unwanted berry and juniper bushes that must yield to a future tree farm. Five wheelbarrow loads of "weeds" was the daily assignment. As the fruit ripened into sweet, red strawberries, progress halted. Not even the oldest could envision the legion of pine trees that danced in my husband's head. Cousin Jimmy was posted at the crest of the hill to warn of the approach of "Uncle Thpencer," while the others crawled among the berries, knees and chins stained with the juices. As the shock of red hair rose over the hill, the child army dove back into its labors, stained hands clasping the roots to wrench them out of the earth like a prickly devil out of their breasts. With the demise of the berries, "lot" became a dirty word, and even the rusty-nail boards appealed, by contrast.

Denailing or berrying, the clothes got dirty. I gave up the struggle of translating French poetry while a soap opera squawked on the laundromat TV, and accepted a friend's gift of a hand-cranked washer that had lain rusting in a basement for two decades. We got it churning each morning. Just before I left for class, the children would file past to hurl dirty socks and under-wear into the sudsy whirlpool. Afterward I dashed off to the campus, making the transition to French en route. Washing machine became machine *à laver* as I explained to my classmates why I looked as though I'd just been washed up on a Tidal wave.

No blue jeans were allowed in the wash until they were ready to walk in by themselves, and then they proved too much for the frail machine. Once a week, kids and jeans were removed in one piece to the lake. Grandmother loved to tell how she was entertain-ing a group of college trustees at a fancy yard party when the Cornwall wagon squealed to a halt and out poured seven dirty kids, each with a bar of soap, followed by a yapping black Lab. The menagerie swept past the startled guests and headed for the lake, then plunged in — clothes, dog, and all — and within seconds had the water whipped to a frenzied foam. The yard guests retired indoors at once for their strawberry shortcake.

The work-play routine nourished the spirits by day, but at night, in the privacy of their beds as we made the kissing rounds, there was now and then a glistening eye and a whispered plea: "Is my daddy coming home soon?"

"Well, he's improving every day," was the answer, while the white lie tugged at our insides. Chuck was still alive — if the mere act of breathing meant improvement. And in a way it did, we rationalized, as he had small chance of survival at the time of impact, and each breath thereafter was an impulse toward life.

Ten days after the cousins' arrival, there was a sharp reversal. An IBM executive called one night to ask Spence and his mother to come at once; a plane would meet them in Burlington. Throwing together a toothbrush, change of underwear, and a set of dark clothing, they headed for the airport. Halfway there, the old Ford sighed and ran out of gas. Overhead a plane blinked low in the sky. While his mother wrung her hands in the front seat, Spence flagged down a passing motorist. Within minutes he was back again with a can full of gas, along with a police escort, and the Ford ground on up Route 7.

Though it was Mother Wright's first flight, and only a short time after her son's crash, she strapped herself bravely into the seat and watched Lake Champlain wink away as the small six-seater took off into the night sky. At two a.m. mother and son were rushed by limousine to the hospital, where they found Chuck in traction, but conscious: his handsome face pale as death, yet the eyes sky-blue and focused on his mother's face. The lips trembled into a smile. But the movement was all in the eyes and mouth. From the broken neck down there was a terrible stillness. The spinal cord had been severed. He had a day or two at most, according to the doctors. His wife summoned a minister.

Yet he made it through that first crisis — and by sheer will, said the nurses. Several days later Spence and his mother returned to Cornwall, the mourning clothes still folded into their bags. It was then she showed us the letter she'd received from Chuck the morning of his accident: "See you Thursday, Mother," it read, "unless we call or have some unplanned delay."

Back at the Broken House, relieved in Spence's absence of nail and shrub pulling, pea soup and outdoor peeing, the children had organized into a kids' army, of which Gary, as the oldest and most visionary, was self-appointed general, complete with cherrywood staff (he'd always admired Virginia Graham's) and a hierarchy of underlings. There were Colonel Mark and Major Chris Wood, tattered baseball caps pulled down over their butch haircuts; sergeants Lesley and Sandy; privates Jimmy and Donald, and Jane Collier from next door. And there was Bonnie, a moist-eyed stray who'd attached herself to the end of the ranks and was made a corporal, a red flag tied to her tail. The privates' complaint that she was only a dog, and shouldn't be of higher rank than themselves, fell on deaf ears.

Peter Dempewolf and one or two other neighbor children who hadn't yet joined up, served as the "enemy." General Gary, a budding Machiavellian, would call on Lesley to lure the outlaws to the tree house, and under cover of branches the Army would pelt them with apples. This went on until one day Peter was felled by a green apple. His eyes glazed over on impact, he went out cold. After that, the Army itself was forced to lie low for a time.

To qualify for the Army you had to walk an eight-by-eight beam over the grinning teeth of farm machinery in the Woods' barn, then leap fifteen feet into the hay below, while General Gary stood with folded arms and a leer on his face that pronounced you "chicken" if you so much as blinked. Gary himself never had to run the gauntlet. It wasn't until years later, when his father enlisted his help in roofing the house, that Gary's acrophobia was discovered — the General was deathly afraid of heights. His reputation as a lad with vision prevailed, however, and no one, other than his sister Lesley, who knew just how far she could go, dared contradict him with impunity.

After Peter and the others passed the trial-by-beam and were accepted into the Army, the gang fanned out into the neighborhood at large in search of a new enemy. One hot day, the entire afternoon was spent lying in the sumac to spy on a grumpy neighbor and record his movements as he passed in and out of his house. When Lesley dared complain of heat and thirst she was told to stay there and "suck rocks." If she let the enemy out of her sight, General Gary warned, she would spend the night on the spot — at the risk of bears, skunks, spooks, and other unnamables that were known to frequent the area.

Terrified, in spite of her resolve to become a "witch" and get back at her brother, she remained, while the enemy sat comfortably in his house and consumed a tuna fish salad and a cold beer. Sweating and miserable on her stomach, forgotten by her general, Sergeant Lesley was at last returned under orders of her father, and scolded for missing her supper. She rushed at once down to the hut, where the Chiefs of Staff lay scheming on their cots.

"I quit your stupid old Army!" she screamed.

"You're court-martialed!" bawled the commanding officer, banging his staff.

Szzz-zzz-zz, came their father's shrill whistle, and out went the lights — controlled from above — leaving the ex-sergeant to stumble back up the slope on the soles of her stubborn little feet. She fell out of the Army, she recalled years later, like an angel out of Heaven — a Heaven full of male angels with cherrywood staffs.

In the end she was to see General Gary himself, like a Mac-Arthur grown too big for his boots, subjected to a higher authority. An apple foray that swept through the neighborhood, shattering several windows, evoked a series of phone calls. The Lane sisters, in particular, made it clear that they didn't care for a troop of grimy-faced urchins peering through their kitchen window while they prepared a beef stew (witches' brew, said the guerillas). The General himself was soundly thrashed by a higher authority, and the Army put on N.C. (neighborhood clean-up). Officers and privates alike ran trash and yanked up dandelions for the neighbors, while the defected Lesley, put to work "on general principle," marched a broom grimly through the shop.

If Gary had a vision, it was inherited from his father, whose mission was every bit as radical in its own way. "Lift that beam! Uproot that bush!" he sang out, while in his mind's eye ten thousand trees sprang up into a tree farm, and the old barn metamorphosed into a five-room shop. And since he was bigger and older, the Army ultimately disintegrated into a source of manual labor, a tool in the redhaired patriarch's fiery clutches.

Because of the delicate balance perhaps — the Sword of Damocles dangling over the childhood games; the competitive spirit, like an Olympic torch, burning under the finger of Discipline — it was a Huck Finn, fantasy summer for the children. By the end of August they were one family. If baby Catharine wet her bed, Sandy helped change the sheets. If Mark mourned his parents, Lesley comforted.

For the adults, of course, the summer was less than idyllic. Enervating, rather, with the calls back and forth to Rochester, the ebb and flow of Chuck's heartbeat, although his spirit never flagged. In the end, even the doctors had to agree that this is what saved him — the same kind of sheer guts that made the children tread the beam over dangerous machinery and leap into a void below, trusting it would somehow cushion their bodies. A foolhardy pilot betrayed Chuck Wright's trust, but the crash failed to put out the light.

On Labor Day we drove the cousins home to their mother in Wappingers Falls, where she'd returned to reorder her life. Chuck would live, but only intensive therapy would tell if he could ever urge any movement out of the rigid limbs. By December he was moved closer to home, to Rusk Institute in New York City.

When Spence and I went to visit him there shortly before Christmas, he greeted us with a broad smile and a bet on the Green Bay Packers. To look at the giant head of blond curls, he might have been at home, in bed with a cold. But under the blankets there was an inutterable stillness. As we entered the room, a young man in the next bed stared at us bleakly, then turned his face to the wall. "He dove into an empty swimming pool," Chuck whispered. "Now his girlfriend has deserted him." We looked at the portrait of Barbara and the three grinning children on Chuck's bed table, and nodded. The young man died several weeks later, while today Charles Wright is the country's longest-lived quadriplegic.

Back at the hotel we were greeted by a shrilling telephone. It was Grandmother, up in Vermont. The temperature had plunged to ten below zero, the pipes had frozen. "Even the wee-wee froze in the chamber pots," she whimpered. In the background we heard the piping of childish voices.

"Oh dear," I said, hearing our weekend away from home and kids begin to crumble. "We'll come right back, then."

Spencer grabbed the phone. "Mother!" he shouted. "Call the plumber. If you can't get him, climb into your long underwear. We're not coming home until tomorrow night!"

"Well," she said weakly. "I suppose, if we have to — "

"Thanks, Mother," said her son, and plunged into a description of our visit with Chuck. "He won the bet, too," he told her. "He always does. Cost me five bucks!"

At the end Mother Wright was urging us to spend a third night in the city. "You'll need it," she said. "We can hang on one more day (her voice growing smaller), I think."

Sounds of Protest:
Pot, Politics, and Pine Trees

THE RESTLESSNESS of the sixties strained beyond college youth and the newspaper accounts of revolutionary machismo and into our personal lives. One of the radical Chicago Seven, we discovered, had a cottage four doors north of us at Lake Dunmore. We only heard of his exploits through the grapevines that divided our camp from his. But all the running around and tossing grenades in the name of Truth at once titillated and frightened us.

At Proctor our most docile students metamorphosed overnight into antiheroes who wrote scathing editorials about the school (now become the "establishment") and arrived at class in defiant ignorance of all assigned work. They squatted by day on the school green to protest the Vietnam War; sat cross-legged at night in the dim shroud of their bedspread-tented rooms to pass a smoking pipe of marijuana or hashish. During one Tuesday faculty meeting attended by a narcotics agent, the stuff was passed hand to hand and sniffed by masters and wives alike, none of us daring to look at one another, knowing what we must do, even to our most brilliant students, should the thick, sweetish aroma come to our nostrils.

There were times when I joined the protestors on the green,

or on stage, directing experimental productions: Heller's "We Bombed In New Haven" or Ionesco's "Rhinoceros," where in the end the populace turns into grunting, snorting, conforming rhinoceri. The boys cheered, but the headmaster announced publicly that such plays were not his "cup of tea." My latter-day rebellion had led me the year before to a summer alone in Paris, at the Sorbonne, for a final push toward my M.A. I was beginning to emerge that year from the diaper pail, as damp and smelly in my own way as the boys with their "weed." Paris to me was Utopia, Shangri La, a world of gold domes and free spirits. Although at times I was lonely, I never went back on my dream.

The summer of my dissent was only made possible by the cheerful pressing-on of my husband and the help of my older sister, Grace, who emerged from her kindergarten into a squealing hive of nieces and nephews. As back-up, Sandy and Sue Hemenway, teen-age daughters of Spence's cousin Paul, split the summer between them — and at times, they claimed, their psyches. Fourteen-year-old Sue had the most traumatic half. When Lesley began to sink after a prolonged swim at the lake, it was tiny Sue who thrashed through the waters in a red tank suit to drag her ward to shore. Shortly afterward she was witness to the demise of Gary's cat, Willy. Suicide, Lesley called it — what man or beast, she said, could withstand her brother's tortures? The highway death was the more unbearable to the latter because Lesley's cat, Carmen, who was trotting along behind Willy, lived to savor the chipmunk Willy was carrying in his maw.

But the chief conflict lay between Grace and Virginia Graham. Labeling Grace a "softie," Virginia marched across the lawns each morning to bang on the old stove grates (Spencer having slipped back into his old ways) and oversee the children's breakfast. "Go up and get dressed," she'd scold when they arrived in their ripped pajamas. Grace held her own, though, when it came to politics. It was the summer of the Johnson-Goldwater election. An arch conservative, Virginia would plant herself each night in front of our TV set. When Johnson's face appeared on the screen she'd lean forward on her cherrywood staff to waggle a scornful finger at "That awful man! That war mongerer!" Goldwater, at least, would keep the peace and upgrade the economy. Hadn't he been a businessman? Owned his own department store?

"I read somewhere," responded Grace, "that Goldwater once sent a dead mouse up to the third floor in the change tube. The poor woman who opened it almost died."

"Smart business practice," said Virginia. "Kept those lazy salesgirls on their toes."

Goldwater was as good as "in," she proclaimed, glancing at liberal Grace out of the corner of her eye: "He won the Vermont primary, didn't he? As Vermont goes, so goes the nation."

"He won the Republican primary, not the election," said Grace. "Besides, it's not Vermont, it's Maine. As Maine goes — "

"Never mind," said Virginia.

Virginia was also for Miller, Goldwater's running mate, until she discovered he was against Medicare. "Ah can never accept that!" she said.

"Well, I wouldn't worry, girls," said Spencer, coming in on the argument. "You know what Truman said: 'A vice president is about as useful as a cow's fifth tit.' "

"Spensah! There are ladies present!" cried Virginia. She rose up on her staff and paraded off toward the bathroom. "Anyhow," she said over her shoulder, "The word was 'teat,' not — " And she slapped the door shut behind her.

According to Grace, Virginia had an ulterior motive for her frequent visits. She had given up her "machine" due to deteriorating eyesight, and Grace provided wheels — to the relief of neighbor wives, who were summoned almost daily during the winter: "Mar-tha? When you all go in town today, stop for me, will you? I'm out of blue thread." Or, "Ann? I need some pink ribbon. Right now. Honk for me, will y' all?"

And the Broken House was a source of water — fresh, if not plentiful. One of Virginia's cut-rate plumbers, unbeknown to her, had hooked up her water softener the wrong way, resulting in an acrid salty taste. For several years she complained of the "bad water" down her way. Because of her elderly boarding-house charges, she was chary of her water. "Country people don't flush every time," was her credo, one that she continued to observe in our house, according to Grace, marching out afterward with a faraway look in her eye as if she were somehow detached from it all.

Oblivious of the discord inside the house, Spence went on with his summer projects, expanding the kitchen several feet to the rear, laying a marble walk, and replacing the saggy back porch with a new one. He had it all but nailed in when his gold wedding ring slipped through a crack and into the bedrock below. The ring never came to light; he likes to think that to this day it shines on some small creature's nest, a glint of sun in a dark hole.

To complete the walk he declared a Marble Day. Attaching a second-hand trailer to the old station wagon, he loaded up kids and dog and drove to the site of the Vermont Marble Company. The mill was long since defunct and the marble lay in broken pieces on the banks of the New Haven River. The children were assigned, according to age and size, to drag the pieces up and heave them into the trailer.

At the end of the day Spence yelled "All aboard!" and car and trailer lurched off along the dirt road. It was already twilight —Spence's foraging expeditions invariably climaxed in the night, rails or beams sticking out like ghostly limbs from flatbed trucks or trailers. Seven-year-old Donald was lurching along in the rear with Lesley. They squatted in the back of the laden trailer at opposite ends "to help balance the weight," as their dad had requested. It was the first time Don had been allowed to ride in the trailer. His carroty hair on end in the wind, he spurred on his marble steed. In a mile or two, he knew, at the main road, he would have to disembark and ride the rest of the way in the car, where his father, Gary, and the dog were already sitting.

"So when do I get off, anyway?" he called to his sister.

"Pretty soon," she said. "Better start getting ready."

The trailer was rounding a wide, slow bend in the road. Don crept to the edge of the trailer, crouched there on his knees, his hands clutching the splintery sides. It would be the briefest of stops, his father had warned. He must be ready, prove he could handle himself as well as the older two. "Say when!" he screeched.

She claimed afterward she never dreamed he'd do it, that she was only teasing him. That it was Gary's grinning face in the rearview mirror that drove her on. But just as the vehicle was rounding a bend, the dust whooshing up in their faces, their father, grim-faced, at the wheel: "Now!" Lesley cried. And giving a blood-curdling yell, the boy leaped.

"Better stop, Dad. Donald's in the road," Gary murmured to his father.

Jamming on the brakes, Spence made his own leap out of the car to find his son in the gravel — no limbs broken as far as he could see, but the boy was in shock and bleeding from numerous cuts. His sister was hunched, whimpering, in the trailer. "Everybody out!" Spence bawled, while the dog howled, her front legs jammed against the back window.

"But Dad — what did I do?" said Gary.

"You were signaling in the mirror. You know you were!" Lesley accused.

Bent over the hood of the car, the older pair suffered three whacks each on the rear end from Father's calloused hand. The sight of it brought Donald out of shock and limping into the front seat, where he rode in silence, like a martyred Christ child, the rest of the way home. His limp persisted for another month until I arrived, and then it miraculously disappeared.

Each day that summer, it seemed, brought a fresh crisis. I unfolded letters full of catastrophic tales from Spence, which I read between bouts of Victor Hugo or Rabelais. Sometimes the subject was Grace:

> July 7: The kids got hyper coming back from the lake last night, and started wrestling in the car — Gary the ringleader, of course. I had to have the old lineup, outside on Route 53. Your sister was all in a tizzy. "Not the little one!" she kept screaming. "Spare the little one!"

> July 31: Your sister seems to think she has to defend your rights around here. Today I gave Sandy a whack on the rear end to get her moving into the shop — customers were waiting. Sandy laughed, of course. But Grace came running up behind: "Remember, Spencer," she said, her lips all pursed, "You're a married man!"

Or Virginia:

> July 18: Today the white angora Meon got off the
> rope V. ties her on and went up the tree again. The damn
> fool likes to climb up, but then panics and sits howling in
> the top branch. V. comes shrieking over and waving her
> stick just as I'm holding a ten-foot beam in place in the new
> kitchen: "Meon! My baby Meon!" Had to send Lesley to
> rescue the fool cat. Got her face all scratched up in the
> bargain where the beast panicked half-way down.

> August 6: Big disaster today. Windy as hell, two
> weeks without rain. And Virginia decides to burn. Henry
> and I are laying the porch — no one goes in or out until it's
> done — and then come cries of Fire! We look over to see
> smoke billowing up from Virginia's place. Sky's black with
> it, sirens screaming. We grab our brooms, arrive with the
> fire trucks. Whole yard's ablaze. V. doing a fire dance in
> the yard, howling like a banshee. It seems she'd put a
> match to her trash bucket, out in the tall grass behind the
> barn. "Get it out!" she's yelling, "Don't you dare let it get
> my house! Get it out!" Well she was lucky this time. They
> got it out. But the Grand Dame was fined $25 by Chief
> Shorkey, and at that, she got off easy.

The letters would usually end with a tale or two of the children's escapades or the latest pump-out by a customer: "I'm putting up a sign now: Pls Jiggle the Handle after U Flush." And then, tugging on my guilt as he had in the days of the Bread Loaf Writers' Conference — although he could hardly rush me back to Cornwall for an hour or two's interlude: "Every night I sit outside under the big maple with a six-pack and my corncob and look up at the stars, and think of how much I miss you, and what we'll do when you come home. I've got some pretty good ideas, and hope you do too."

I came home in late August on my "flying carpet," as a custom's official dubbed the flea-market Persian rug I clutched under one arm. I descended into a house full of neighbors, at a party staged by the children. Two-year-old Cathy blinked up at me as if I were another customer come to use the facilities. "Is that my mommy?" she asked her sister, and then, as I knelt down to her, dissolved into tears. I found Spence in bed, of course, resting up for my homecoming. His alarm hadn't gone off, he said.

"But I'm the guest of honor," I reminded him as he reached out for me. A babble of voices rose up through the cracks in the floor.

"Well, they can do without you for five more minutes."

"I think they'll have to," I said. And sank down beside him on the bed.

Gary's True Dissent began in the mid-sixties when we started the tree farm. For seventy-five dollars Spence had purchased three thousand red pine seedlings on the assurance of the county forester that they were the "best" Christmas trees. He soon discovered that the long, slippery needles would never hold a piece of tinsel or a glass ornament. Next time, he wisely purchased a thousand two-year-old scotch pine and balsam fir, which arrived in forty small bundles. He transported the children up to the lot and lined them up with spades and buckets.

"These trees will grow into your college educations," he told them.

"Those twigs?" said Gary, peering sceptically into the bucket. "Who wants a college education, anyway?"

"I do," piped Catharine, thinking a college education some kind of holiday.

Gary looked down at his baby sister and guffawed. "You'll never go to college. You can't learn anything."

That winter he'd begun the child's training as an Olympic speed skater. The gold medal he promised her would reflect on him, of course, as her coach. Twice a day during the Christmas break he kept her out on the orchard pond until she completed two hundred circles. When she'd sink down on the ice, exhausted, he'd drag her up and prod her off again. After three weeks of giddy circling, she sat down for the last time, tears mixing with the grime on her face:

"I don't think I want any gold medal," she sobbed.

"Well, I'm sorry for you," he said. And turned on his heel, leaving the ingrate to stumble home alone. She'd been a keen disappointment to him.

No one dared quit, though, under the tree farmer's aegis. It was a veritable rite of spring. We were all made to come. I told the children about the old days when trees were believed to be the lairs of good spirits. "Knock three times after giving your wish," I said, "and it'll come true."

Spence nodded. "Listen to your mother," he said.

"I wish I were out playing baseball," said Gary, knocking on a red pine. And then looked properly sceptical as he found himself still there with a shovel in his hand.

Don and Lesley lugged buckets heavy with six inches of water and fifty seedlings while the groaning Gary dug holes and poked in the "dumb twigs." The tips had to face ten degrees north, their father explained: the sun would ultimately straighten them up. We took turns stamping them in while Cathy trotted behind to sprinkle woodchips around the stems.

"That's a tree farm? That's all there is to it?" Gary said, standing on the crest of the hill to survey a hillside full of rocks and green twigs listing northward.

His father kept a wise silence. His older son was unaware of the coming hours and months of back-breaking mowing and the shearing of ten thousand Christmas trees, and then fifteen thousand as the tree farmer swung into high gear. "Dance the Highland Fling around a fresh Scotch Pine," we would advertise twelve years later. "$5.25, any size. Tag early. U cut."

A few years later the boy rebelled altogether. One night at school he and another lad got into a bottle of vodka in our pantry while we were sipping martinis at a Proctor Academy trustees' meeting. Unable to contain their exuberance, the pair leaped up onto the stage of the Saturday evening movie and did a frenetic dance in front of the larger-than-life bosom of Raquel Welch. The next day they were brought before the headmaster, and as faculty sons, cited as examples of flagrant misbehavior. Much to everyone's astonishment in a day of hashish and LSD, they were expelled.

Gary transferred to the local high school, with the headmaster's promise that he might return the next fall if he proved himself. What hurt the most was that he had to give up the varsity hockey team. There was some consolation, though, in the fact that now his vacations were different from his father's, and he'd miss the spring tree planting. And he would stay alone at the Broken House during his winter break and attend the Middlebury-University of Vermont hockey game. Gold medals still shone in his eyes, if not in Catharine's; to play with the UVM "Cats" was all his dream.

This year UVM beat the Middlebury Panthers in a last-minute upset. Although Middlebury had its arch rival 5-3 well into the third period, the Cats pumped in three goals in the last minutes of play to skate to a 6-5 victory. The place was a bedlam, the Panthers unable to give up a victory snatched from them as untimely as MacDuff from his mother's womb. In the last moments of play a personal vendetta broke out between two players, and everyone, players and spectators alike, leaped into the fray. The last Gary recalls as he watched with glee was the sight of the elderly Lane sisters, always great hockey fans, trying to press their way out the door. Before they could exit, they were knocked down themselves. Marguerite, he claimed, struggled, shrieking, with a male freshman who'd been catapulted into her lap, and who in turn was straining to pull her up. At last the ladies made it through the door, and yanking skirts and hairdos into place, they left the arena, their "hockey" henceforth confined more sensibly to the radio by-plays.

The following summer, exhausted from our struggles with rebelling offspring and students, we sank our combined salaries into the only new car we've ever owned — a green Ford station wagon — left the shop with Aunt Grace and Virginia Graham (one more rope in their tug-of-war), packed up tents and four kids, and headed west.

Our tents teetered on the banks of the Missouri and Mississippi, trembled on the hanging cliffs of the Rockies, leaked under the fury of a Kansas thunderstorm. We had mountain stew — a mix of hamburger, beans, and onion — for breakfast, lunch, and dinner. Lesley lost a shoe at each campsite and in the end went barefoot. Donald fell through the rocks of a California gorge and was rushed to the hospital for nineteen stitches. A bear threatened our tent in Vancouver and was fended off by Spence and Gary with a baseball bat. Still, it was a carefree summer that brought us together as a family — not just children with parents, but wife with husband. Only now and again as we sat outside our tents gazing into a prairie sunset did we wonder what was going on back in Cornwall: if the trees were growing in the August drought, and how the shop was faring in the hands of Grace and Virginia.

"Another election this summer," I said one evening to Spence. "They'll be at each other's throats again."

"Never mind," he said. "They'll survive. And so will the shop."

"Speaking of home — we'll have to buy a new stove when we get back. Virginia broke the last grate the morning we left, getting us up."

"Uh oh. And we just bought a new car."

"Time for supper," I said. "Mountain stew. Live it up."

Home to Old Cornwall

"EA-ZY DOES IT. Lift your end, Donald. Lift, I said!"

It was June of 1971. The boys were on either end of a coffinlike box, their backs bent with the weight of it. The traffic along Route 30 slowed down to watch.

"Make Gary stop pulling back on it, Dad."

"Who, me?" said Gary. "Oh. I thought we were taking it into the shop."

"Bananas," his father said. "Now get it in the house."

The boys deposited the grandfather clock in the middle of the living room. It was packed in the same box in which it had crossed the Atlantic a century and a half before, on the same boat with Spence's great-great grandmother. The ten-foot "coffin" might have contained Henry the Eighth and his six wives. The clock stood tilted between the two boys, six inches too tall for the room.

"Dad," Gary said, "we're going to have to cut a hole for it in the ceiling."

"I told them it wouldn't go in there. But they wouldn't listen," said Mother Wright from her rocking chair.

"In the dining room, then," said Spencer, hot and weary from the move. "I'm not drilling any damn hole."

"Anyway, you can't," I said. "That's Clarissa's closet above there. She has a right to her privacy."

"You and your dumb ghost," Gary muttered. But he said no more about drilling the hole.

I watched them shove aside their grandmother's blanket chest to make room for the clock. Ten chairs were crowded around a four-foot harvest table. Books lay in heaps on the floor, with no room for the bookcases. Our convertible sofa jammed the doorway into the hall. There were now five sofas in the house.

We'd made the final break from academia, come home to Vermont for a second life. A change of space, I called it. We'd work for ourselves, none other — although we'd miss the students, and would welcome them in Cornwall as they dropped by to reminisce. We had no savings. But there were the house, the shop, and the fifteen acres on Cider Mill Road. The headmaster of our school had just retired with little more than his clothes and his scrapbook. "Will the richer man please stand up?" I said. And my husband raised his arms in victory.

Only Catharine would be with us year-round. The others would return to their private schools (the boys at Proctor, Lesley at Northfield-Mt. Hermon), on scholarship. I would run the shop and write while Spence tried his hand, like his father of old, selling on the road. We would dine on rice and tofu. I would wear Indian skirts, run naked around the house in the early morning. It was to be a dream fulfilled.

"There's a roast in the oven. Turn it on, will you?" said Mother Wright from her chair.

"Mother," said Spence. "There's going to be an auction."

Her eyes brightened. "Where?" she said.

"Right here. And half this house is going into it. You and Nancy can decide which half."

"Nonsense," she said, and went back to her rocking.

In September she moved up from the lake a week ahead of schedule: "I mean, since you're here," she said as the boys struggled behind with her color TV and boxes of food, heaps of clothing draped over their arms.

"Oh dear. I just bought material for new green ones," she said as she watched me hang up my old kitchen curtains of beige homespun.

In October Aunt Evelyn arrived, on schedule. (It was two years before her attack of old bones.) She clomped into the house, a cigarette trembling between two fingers. The four sofas (we'd gotten rid of one by then) were soon plump with cigarette ash. So was her bed.

"You'd better stop her smoking in bed," I warned Spence. I began a practice of storing my manuscripts in the refrigerator —until one day I found the pages of my new novel stuck together with maple syrup, and transferred them to the freezer.

For a few weeks Aunt Evelyn and I raced each other to the shop whenever a car pulled in; then sensibly, I gave up and let her take over (Virginia Graham had moved downcountry with the Fullers, and we missed her). Foggy glasses perched on the end of her long nose, Auntie would occasionally trip into the living room, where I'd set up my typewriter, and ask me to check a price. "Don't know why they write 'em so damn small," she grumbled one morning, thrusting a pottery ashtray between me and my manuscript.

" 'They' is me, Auntie," I said, leaving off my novel in mid-sentence. "Why can't you just ask the customer? This is Vermont, not New York."

"Well, she couldn't read it either."

The price sticker in the center of the ashtray, I saw, had been stubbed out by something that looked suspiciously like a cigarette.

"Those goddamn chipmunks," she said, peering closely at it, "always smoking up a storm."

"You're impossible, Auntie," I said, and followed her out to the shop, my immortal words popping like bubbles in the wake of her belly laugh.

In November Adèle Jones arrived for two weeks. A sister Pi Phi to Ruth, class of '22, Adèle was a tall, thin, compassionate woman in an Eva Gabor red wig. She had recently retired from running a Hamburger Hut in the throbbing heart of New York City. The hamburgers never halted her daily visit, back in the sixties, to my brother-in-law Charles's bedside at Rusk Institute.

Adèle and Ruth relieved me of the cooking. Like true "sisters," they were intimate and inimical at alternate moments. When they weren't cooing over snacks in the kitchen, they were arguing over how many onions to put in the meatloaf or how to pare the carrots for the stew they planned for dinner.

Carrots should be pared down finely with a peeler, said Ruth, a purist.

A quick scrape with a knife, that's all, insisted Adèle, drawing on her Hamburger Hut days.

"Throw the goddamn carrots in the pot and be done with it," Aunt Evelyn bawled from the dining room sofa.

A fifth wheel on a vehicle that seemed to be foundering in its tracks, I crept back to my typewriter. I put my novel aside until winter, when everyone would be gone, and began work on a short story. In the end my heroine, a handicapped girl brought up in a boys' school, would break loose and head for the tundras of Alaska.

"What do you want for dessert?" Mother Wright peered around the doorway.

"Hm?" I was on the Alaskan Highway, the windows wide, my hair streaming back in the wind.

"For dessert," she repeated. "I thought I'd make an apple strudel. We could have ice cream, but I'd have to go buy it."

"Fine," I said, tilting into my typewriter. "She jammed her braced foot down on the accelerator," I wrote, "and then — "

"She wants apple strudel!" Ruth shouted to Adèle. "I told you she wouldn't want ice cream."

"Stop screaming in there, you two!" screamed Aunt Evelyn. "I can't hear my goddamn radio!"

Shortly after Thanksgiving Aunt Evelyn made a final complaint about the heatless shop: "You can't skin a cat in a deep freeze," she said, and left for West Nyack. "Keep the faith, honey," said Adèle, and yanking her wig on straight, she departed for her city apartment.

In January Spence and I settled down to cultivate our dreams. Mother Wright was still with us — she'd made her reservations late and wouldn't head south until February. But with no one to argue with, she spent the days reading or napping in her chair, saving all her words for nighttime, when Spence sat down to add

up the commissions he'd earned selling Bancroft tennis rackets or
Fawn Grove pants.

"Take off those pants right now and I'll mend them," she'd tell
him, relieving me (happily) of yet another household duty. "You'll
never sell a tennis racket when you look like a bum off the soup
kitchen line."

"I'll never sell enough anyway," he said, reading off his sales of
the week. Sam's Sports in Bethel: ninety-nine dollars and two
cents. Leicester Four Corners: fifty-six dollars and fifty-six cents,
Lazarus Department Store: one hundred three dollars and no
cents. Out of the above he'd receive a ten percent commission.
"Twenty-five dollars and fifty-eight cents," he announced. "Not
counting gas and lunch."

One company had sent no commission at all; its only correspondence was a weekly pep-letter. "Get out there and pitch," it
urged. "We got a new pant that's a honeybell, three gorgeous
colors: rust, fawn and black. Double-seamed pockets and a secret
inside-pocket for that hundred-dollar bill. Who's going to pick that
one? Warn 'em about the ladies, though, ha ha."

"Lemme at that pocket," I said, lunging for my husband, while
Mother Wright gazed into the photographic splendor of *House
Beautiful.*

"How about a Virginia ham for Sunday dinner?" she said.
"With yams. Here's a marvelous recipe."

"You'll have to buy it," I said, my shop contribution for the
week being $9.90. "And pick up a big box of cornflakes while you're
at it. For Monday night's supper."

We never lacked for drink, though. A salesman had inveigled
me into buying two dozen wine-making kits from a company called
(appropriately) Tip and Twinkle. The kit included a gallon jug,
wine yeast (to be used with frozen grape juice), and a handful of
colored balloons. Attached to the jug, these would inflate, then
twenty-one days later go limp, and voilà! The shipment, unpacked
in our kitchen, never reached the shop shelves. Within hours eight
gallons of "Old Cornwall" was gurgling away on the kitchen table.
Unable to wait for the twenty-one days to elapse, Spence popped
the balloon on the twentieth and called over the neighbors for a
tasting party.

Mother Wright's attention was soon diverted from the state of her son's pants to the slur in his words. The wine was too strong, she said. She felt tiddly herself after a sip.

He didn't feel a thing, he countered, after four glasses. "Of course you don't," she said. "That's what I'm telling you."

To settle the question Doc Collier brought over his hydrometer. The wine, he announced, measured 8½ proof. "You see?" she said, though she didn't know eight proof from eighty. "I ought to stay here the rest of the winter and keep an eye on you."

Spencer stashed away the jugs down cellar. In mid-February we waved good-bye to Ruth. At seventy-five years old she was still heading south alone, in a four-year-old Plymouth packed to the roof with coats, dresses, Knox hat boxes, and bags full of size eleven shoes. It was an afternoon departure, as she seldom arose before noon. We were all there to say good-bye, including Catharine, waving the cat's paw. Mother's and daughter's eyes watered as Grandmother drove off on what she seemed to consider her Last Journey.

"My will is in the safe deposit box!" she hollered as she pulled out of the driveway. "So is the deed to the camp. Write to me now, write!" And waving frantically through the open window, a moist-eyed woman in a purple felt hat pitched over one eyebrow, she wobbled off down the highway.

We wallowed in the freedom of that first midwinter: no deadlines, no students banging on our door in the middle of the night, no heavy roasts with gravy for dinner. No money either — although we had a windfall in early March when Hope Ryan, Ruthven's mother and the Indian army colonel's widow, came over to order a table and chairs for a cottage she was building on Lake Champlain. Gary, now a high school senior, helped deliver, and came home with a five-dollar tip and a new job as her Cornwall gardener. Apparently he'd trampled a lilac bush while trying to move in the table, and paused to coax it upright again. That chance embrace led to a new career — one for which he was eminently unsuited.

A bulwark of the Cornwall Garden Club, Hope was dubbed The Major-General by Virginia Graham because, according to

Virginia, she hired help to grow her flowers. A series of gardeners, which soon included Gary, pruned her shrubs and roses and tapped her maple trees — not for the sap but because she felt it was "good for them." When they had nothing else to do they paraded past her windows with pitchforks over their shoulders. Gary managed to yank up, in his blind ardor, several rosebushes and half her iris bed — to the satisfaction of the Lane sisters next door, who were arch rivals for the Ineffable Iris. Convinced that the lad was Hope's secret weapon, the reason she took so many Garden Club "firsts," they conspired to win him away.

The sisters lived next door in a little green house that served as the site of the Cornwall Weather Station, which had been in the family for a century, and was used by their nephew, Judge Stuart Witherell, Cornwall's town historian, to record the daily weather. Jessie, the younger, was as short and plump and cheerful as Marguerite was tall and thin and frequently "out of sorts." The latter had her reasons, of course: while Jessie taught kindergarten downcountry all her working years, it was Marguerite's lot to cut short her career as a domestic science teacher at Beaver College and come home to care for an ailing mother. The mother lived another twenty years, passing on two weeks before the 1950 hurricane that blew the front porch up over the roof and knocked over the weather station (reporting "no weather" at all that day). Jessie came home then to take over the garden, while Marguerite tended house.

One Saturday in July, Hope Ryan looked out her window to see her employee on the "other" side of the fence, clipping bushes, with Jessie Lane directing his hand as if he had a crayon in it and not a pair of gardening shears. Hope raised the window a crack:

"Over here now, Gary," came Jessie's voice. "Clip this little fellow. That's it. Uh oh, not too much now, just an inch. Good lad!"

"It's too much!" cried Marguerite from the porch, a stirring spoon in her hand. "Now she can see into our windows."

"She certainly can!" Hope yelled, shoving the window all the way up. "And that's my fellow you've got. He's supposed to be working over here!"

There was a brief consultation between Jessie and her weekend gardener. Then Gary went on clipping while Jessie hollered over the fence: "He doesn't work for you Saturdays. He's free to come here."

"He should be home then, helping his mother," Hope yelled back, and slammed the window.

Gary grew indispensable to the Lane sisters, who were then in their eighties. It didn't seem to matter that he couldn't tell a peony from a plum tree. He could shoot a mean hockey puck, and the sisters were still fans, if only via the radio. A six-foot center on the UVM hockey team, Gary was a good-luck piece, a kind of rabbit's foot. He could do no wrong. If he pulled up a primrose — well, they needed thinning anyway. If he stumbled and broke something inside the house, unused to the dark (the shades were drawn year-round to keep the heat in during the winter and out in the summer) Jessie would say, "It's all right. That cup was old as the hills, full of cracks. I'm glad it broke. Good for you, Gary!"

After Gary cleaned out the basement, sweeping the debris and old bottles from around the pipes, he suddenly found himself an authority on plumbing. "Do you think that's why the water pressure has been so low, Gary? Because of all the debris around the pipes?"

"Well — ," he'd say, and nod his head a little the way his father did under the hood of a car when he knew nothing of its inner workings. "Oh, Gary's solved the problem!" Jessie would burble.

He was up at a summer hockey camp the day the aged joint gave way and the pipes burst in a roar of water that rivaled Otter Creek Falls. The sisters had to settle for a local plumber, who managed to stem the tide. Tools and pipes were strewn all over the basement floor the following Saturday as Gary reported for work.

"Gary's here!" the sister screamed in unison. "Oh thank heaven!" Grabbing his arms, they shoved him toward the cellar steps. "Here he is, Mr. Billings, he knows all about our pipes. He'll show you what to do now." And they hurried back to their cups of tea, leaving their employee to face the master plumber who'd repaired the Broken House toilet when Gary's diapers were still being scraped into it.

Fortunately, it was Charlie Willson, not Gary, who helped with my first full-time garden that summer. I took at once to his method of heaving in the seed and heaping on the dirt, regardless of instructions. And everything grew. "The lettuce is up!" I screeched at Spence as he staggered out of the car, a dozen tennis rackets under his arms. "And something else. Little, thick, green things like four-leaf clovers!"

"Radish," he said wearily. "They always come up first."

"Oh," I said, racing back to fall on my knees and gaze at it: something I'd planted, thrusting up through the June earth like a baby escaping the womb. Around me was the thick, good smell of dirt, and bees humming in the locust blossoms like a heavenly harmony.

The animals loved the garden, too. Our collie, Hester, retired from the school hockey rink, where she nipped the rear ends of the players as they skated on and off the ice, considered it a substitute playground. Our pet rabbit, Harvey, who had hopped about with impunity at school, became in Cornwall the object of various vendettas as he pirouetted from garden to garden, including my own, crunching on cauliflower and cabbage leaves.

One day Catharine brought home two baby Pekin ducks. The second night the female was snatched out of the backyard runway by an owl. We built a wooden fortress for the male, who metamorphosed into a great white bird and bosom member of the family. He ran flapping out to meet the school bus each afternoon, and followed me everywhere: to the clothes line, where he plucked the underpants out of the laundry basket; to the back garden, where he spread his soft white feathers over the tiny seedlings and every few seconds dropped on a little fertilizer. He never discriminated in that regard, but spread it equally over porch and kitchen floor when he squeezed through with a cat or dog, and in the shop, where he'd waddle about importantly and grab at the customers' legs.

To keep Quack out of shop and garden we got him a mate: a skittish brown Rouen whom Catharine named Felina. Although she quickly became a mate in every sense and each day laid a large white egg that made succulent souffles, she met with one accident after another. She was nibbling the grass outside the shop one day when a carload of long-haired lads let loose a hound dog. Giving a predatory howl, the beast made a dash for Felina, and took her head in its mouth. Quack lunged at the beast, jabbing with his beak and then retreating, like Groucho Marx in a boxing match. The dog's owner ran to call off the fray while I shrieked and Catharine stood paralyzed, her mouth a round O. At last the dog let go and Felina skittered away to her box, her feathers soaked with saliva. She remained there for two days, refusing to lay, as if to punish us for having the shop that brought the dog that almost did her in.

One day a month or so later, when Quack marched out of his box full of his morning song, Felina wasn't able to join him. She would surge out, then arch her neck and pull back in a kind of spasm. The male plunged into the box to peck at her neck. Around the Rouen's neck, we saw, was a loose wire; Quack was attempting to disengage it. Catharine was able at last to clip the wire, and the pair shot out, rejoicing. Quack rushed up to thrust his beak in her neck: "I love you, you silly old duck," she said, and gathered the Pekin's wiggly body into her arms while his gabbling quieted to a soft chuckling.

In the end it was Felina who survived, when Quack waddled out to frolic in the rainwater at the edge of the road, and met his karma. Someone, speeding down the highway, didn't notice — or care — that a white duck was bathing there. There wasn't a mark on the body. But there was no pecking at her cheek as a weeping girl carried her feathery friend into the house.

The ducks' adventures were recorded in detail in the *Addison Independent,* the local weekly for which I became the Cornwall correspondent. At ten cents an inch, I learned to make a mountain out of any molehill. "You don't have to go over Otter Falls in a barrel to make the Cornwall News," I advertised. And the townspeople responded, ringing my telephone off the hook:

Mrs. Maurice Bingham served her first plateful of juicy green peas on June 24.

John Powers has announced that his dump truck is now in solid working condition.

Spotted on a maple tree along Cider Mill Road, collecting March sap, is a chamberpot covered with tinfoil.

A certain local college student was apprehended streaking down Main Street in Burlington. Arriving at the police station, clad only in his birthday suit, he was asked to "produce identification."

Linda and John Coombs report that their phone is working again after one of their puppies chewed through the cord. Last year a rabbit bit through in the same place.

According to Ann Lyon, literary mice abound in Cornwall Library. They have shown particular interest in the archival shelves, and in library cards held by the deceased.

Guest of the Wrights is Evelyn McGregor. For years, en route to New York City, she flashed a picture of Eleanor Roosevelt on her commuter's ticket and got away with it.

When I'd exhausted the family news, I dipped into family history. My efforts spread beyond the newspaper. The fictionalized tale of the fertilized Petticoat Strip and breach-of-promise suit was sent off to the *Saturday Evening Post*. The story was published elsewhere than in that august magazine, but my rejection note appeared in print. Signed by then-editor Julie Nixon Eisenhower just after her Dad was expelled from the White House, the letter was published in *Writer's Digest* magazine. A week later I received the following missive:

Dear Nancy Means Wright,

I am a prisoner in Atticus State Prison. I saw about your Strip story in the Dijest. I am offering you the oportunity to tell my life, you sound like the one to do it. I been through it all, beleive me, booze women pimping, you name it. We could colaborate by mail. You get 15%. I'll expect your answer, send details.

Sincerely,

Ron Gallizone

The first two years of our "second chance" culminated in a trip to New York City to deliver furniture. Spencer was in between sales and real estate then. He was glad to accompany me on a paid vacation, even though it was fall, our favorite season. We were to deliver a complete living room set to a couple on 69th Street. We had driven before in New York, but never with furniture teetering on the roof and hanging out the rear of the station wagon. Entering the city was like (we imagined) being shot out of a rocket. We didn't drive, we were driven, by a cacophony of cabs and trucks. We careened at last into 69th, to be met by a No Stopping sign. We stopped. The cars honked behind us, people shrieked out the windows: "Cancha read the sign?" My ears thundering, I ran into the building. The apartment we were delivering to was on the sixth floor. I rang up. There was no answer. A thousand heartbeats later a doorman appeared to inform us that the couple was out, we were to leave the furniture inside the lobby. I wept with relief.

Outside Spence was unloading, with the help of a teenager who'd happened along. Already a group was gathering to inspect the furniture. "Vermont pine?" a woman asked, peering at a five-foot round extension table. "Geez, they make it right from the trees up there, huh? How much you want for it?" "I'll take those two chairs right now for a hundred bucks," said another, "no questions asked."

"You see the sign there, mister?" bawled a husky voice. "It says No Stopping. That means NO Stopping. No selling on the sidewalks either."

"What are we supposed to do, Officer, throw the stuff out the windows?" Spence yelled, his forehead beaded with sweat. The officer didn't care. He was rounding the block he said, and when he returned he wanted us out of there. He shot on up the street. Then jammed on his brakes and backed up. "Vermont, huh?" he said, eyeing the license plate. He got out of the car. "You ever make 'em on a — you know — pedestal? The wife's been lookin' for one." We handed him a shop brochure, and he started off. "Next time, though," he warned, "don't make it such a production."

"The Wrights' New York production," I told my Cornwall readers in the next issue of the *Independent*, "turned out to be a nonprofit one. Dinner and a night in a city hotel ate up half the proceeds. Then, coming back, the fan belt gave way outside Hoosick Falls, New York. The couple sat helpless by the side of the road while carloads of leaf peepers whizzed by. The Hoosick Garage pocketed the remainder of their gain.

"The day was on the wane," I went on, "as they crept into their own driveway. 'Have you ever seen a maple tree like that in all your life?' He said, gazing up at the autumn glory."

" 'No' She said. 'Never. And look at those mountains!' "

" 'Gezum,' He said. 'Well, come on, Nance. Grab that suitcase. We're home!' "

The Bride Rode a Broomstick (and Other Ups and Downs)

"SOMETHING'S HAPPENED. I'm not Donald any more," our second son told Lesley, his sister-confessor. He was in his sophomore year at the University of Vermont. His dormitory room resembled a witch's cauldron: blue lights dimly illuminated the smoke clouds mushrooming up from a dozen trembly fingers.

"Who are you then — David Bowie?" she said, eyeing the black outfit he wore, the silver sprinkles on his forehead.

"No, no," he moaned. "I can't sleep any more. I can't eat. Touch me. See? Nothing! I can't feel."

"Hamlet's ghost, then," she guessed.

"My heart skips all the time. I need a doctor. Listen: One. Two. There! It's missed again! Hear it?"

"How can I hear it if it's not beating?" asked Lesley. She reminded him of the health insurance we'd dropped to keep them all in school. "They should have kept the insurance and dropped the school," she observed.

"I'll stay," he said, sinking into a chair, a pale martyr, his red hair frizzing about his shoulders.

"You'll go," I said, bursting in on the scene, and rushed him to the hospital emergency room.

"No more coffee," said the doctor after a thorough examination. "No more of whatever else goes on in those dormitory rooms. There's nothing wrong that a little rest and change won't help cure."

"What about my heart?" said Donald, clutching his chest.

The doctor bent his head. "I hear it," he said.

Declaring a moratorium, Donald went west with a friend. Although their car and its contents were stolen by a hitchhiker in Calgary, Alberta, and they were mugged in Vancouver by some friendly locals, our callow Candide returned from his journey a wiser and healthier person. After a year of working with the retarded, for whom he developed an abiding affection, he returned to the world of books — and surprised us by landing on the Dean's List. Then it was his turn to give advice.

"Should I marry him?" Lesley said. "Can you imagine me married? Is it fair to him? What do you think, Donald?"

"But aren't the invitations already out?" he said.

"Do you think that could possibly make any difference?" she cried. "When my whole life's at stake? His, too?"

The Witch's Wedding, we called it. Green-eyed Lesley, who once hid a broomstick in her closet and threatened to turn her siblings into cats and owls, was now promising to ride a broomstick down the aisle. "You'll be sorry you invited all those hundreds of people!"

Three years before, at the age of eighteen, Lesley had earned the money to take a year off before entering Middlebury College. Drawn by the Buddhist East, she crossed the Atlantic alone, to backpack through Europe and the Middle East. I unraveled the bed each night, tossing, imagining her under attack by bears or bandits. "If she reaches Afghanistan," said our orchard friend Ruthven Ryan, "you'd better fly out and get her back."

"But we don't know where she's going," I said, wringing my hands, "until we get a letter. By then she's gone!"

Her letters, though, gave me grist for the Cornwall News mill. "Lesley Wright, who had long dreamed of the lands of spice and honey," I wrote, "had her money, glasses, and return plane ticket stolen while she sat crammed into an Indian train. The final blow came the next night, in Benares, when a monkey reached in the window of her ten-cent hotel room and snatched her supper of fruit and bread."

"In Delhi," read a later installment, "when her money ran out and she was obliged to turn her thoughts homeward, she booked passage to Holland. Turned away at the last minute, she embarked the following day for Istanbul. In the Afghanistan desert they came upon the carcass of the Holland bus, its engine gutted, passengers abandoned when the driver absconded with the fares."

"Later Lesley's bus broke down; the occupants slept in tents by its side. Happily, not bandits but smiling women bore down on them, bearing loaves of bread. The girl last wrote from Teheran, Iran, where the vehicle arrived dragging its rear end like a tin can through the streets."

Not long afterward, our kitchen door flew open and a pale, hank-haired waif appeared, dressed in raggedy Indian shirt and trousers, the skin shrunken on her bones and one (Indian) nickel in her pocket. "Lesley!" I shrieked, and we fell into one another's arms.

In the shop the next week she waited on a charming young photographer, and after Christmas moved out of the college dorm and into his hand-hewn hut. It was quieter there to study, she told her father. There was no waiting to take a shower. (There *was* no shower, only a cracked wooden toilet that pinched if you sat too long.) Her father, who had held up under a year of her Asian adventures, passed out at the news of this latest defection and pitched headlong into the Persian rug.

He was revived with brandy — and her ultimate decision to marry. "But I'm wearing a sheet," she warned. "Maybe holes for the eyes. I'll carry a bouquet of snakes and toadstools."

"The Bride Wore a Broomstick" was the title of a short story I wrote afterward for *Yankee* magazine. "Everyone loves a bride. Except my daughter Jo. The very word makes her bridle," the story began. And ended with the wedding scene, the couple vanishing into an old white Volvo: "Bride and groom are fading shadows on the grass." (Jessie Lane, then a nonagenarian in a nursing home, was shocked by the story: "You told all your secrets," she said, wagging a trembly finger at me.)

The main drama was played out in the Broken House before

the ceremony. We were getting the bride into her "sheet" — actually an Indian gauze dress with lacy neck and fly-away sleeves she'd bought on sale for twenty-seven dollars. The skirt dipped and stretched between ankle and knee. Below, she'd stuck her size six feet into Chinese slippers. She would carry no bouquet, not even toadstools, unless her James carried one, and he demurred. The raw broccoli and cauliflower were all chopped and ready for a vegetarian feast at Grandmother's lake camp. ("Ridiculous," said the latter, and with the help of her sister Florence, who shared the Ashworth passion for food, whipped up three hundred chicken sandwiches anyway.)

The father of the bride was up from his pre-game nap and shaving. He and I would precede Lesley down the aisle. Catharine would light the candles, and the boys perform (more or less) as ushers. Donald was gorgeous in his grandfather's black suit and top hat. Happily, the pants were too long and hid the sneakers he wore. Gary, just home from a softball tournament, was struggling into a suit of his father's.

"I'm not wearing one of those," he warned as Grandmother came at him with a crimson rose.

"Then how will they know you're an usher?" she said.

"Lesley says I'm not an usher. I'm just supposed to point the way down the aisle or something."

"Sure, Let 'em find their own goddamn seats," said Aunt Evelyn, who'd just arrived, her slip hanging an inch below the hem of her thirties dress.

"When do I light the candles?" asked Catharine. "We never practiced that."

"I've never looked so absurd," moaned Gary, squinting into the mirror.

"Shut up. Shut up! All of you!" Lesley screamed. "I'm not getting married!" And she raced out of the house and down the street in her fly-away dress.

CLOSED FOR FAMILY WEDDING read the sign I'd hung on the shop. Afterward Gary added a question mark. "Knock on wood," I said, hammering my knuckles on the shop door, "and hope she'll come to her senses." "She'll come on her broomstick," Gary reminded us.

We greeted our guests as they climbed the church steps. Our old friend Willy Galvin and his wife came in bicentennial costume. "If there isn't a wedding," I suggested, "would you give us a song and dance?"

"It's time," said Murdale, our woman minister. My heart beat in my knees. Inside, top-hatted Donald was rushing the last guest down the aisle, in spite of his sister's instructions. "I can't stop him," said Gary, "he's a wild man." "When do I light the candles?" hissed Catharine.

"Now," said James, the groom, looming up behind. He was stunning in a white suit, a pale rose in his lapel. His face was grave.

Down the aisle we went, to Pachelbel's Canon: first Catharine, in blue, her hands shaking ("I know why the real weddings have bouquets," she whispered). Next came Donald, dehatted, his hair a flaming bush. Then Gary, swaggering, the rose barely visible where he'd stuffed it in his pocket. Spence and I followed, hand in hand.

"Hey, we gotta full house," he said. "There's the Perines, and the Poores. See 'em? Over there."

"Shush," I said as we squeezed into our assigned pew. "This is a wedding."

"You think so?" he said.

"Uh huh. Look!" And there she was, coming down the aisle, the green eyes gazing up and ahead, like a graceful Greek in her wreath of Queen Anne's lace. The wedding guests creaked down into the pews, and then up again: "Morning has bro-ken-n-n," they all sang.

"Gezum, are they going to yank us up and down all through this thing?" Spence whispered.

If the marriage had its ups and downs, so did our lives. "It's time for an 'up,'" said Spence, when the new couple moved in with us for a time, along with two Siamese cats.

"I already have one in mind," I said. When *Seventeen* magazine published my novelette about a Scottish girl's long-ago voyage to America, we took off to Scotland. I would look up my roots.

What I found, though, did not connect. The searcher in Edinburgh blanched as she handed me the ancient record book of Scoonie Kirk. I held it reverently: "I'm anxious to know who my great-grandfather was," I said. "I had this dream that he was a writer. Silly, but — "

"Well, ye'll no find out frae this," she said.

I looked down at the opened page. "Jessie Brown, b. December 24, 1842," the entry read, and then, in thin, spidery letters: "illegitimate."

"There'll be no charge," murmured the searcher.

I determined to turn the news to advantage. "*Green Grow the Lasses*, a saga of strong-minded Scottish women," I wrote in my journal. "Main character: Jessie. Of illegitimate birth. Imagine the notoriety for the poor mother, in a tight little Presbyterian parish."

"Well, leave me out of this one," said Spence, recalling a few years back when my "prep school novel" with himself as anti-hero appeared in paperback from Ace Books. The cover depicted a hairy hand pulling back the curtain where a voluptuous woman was taking a shower. There was no such scene in the book; my heroine was plain Norma Brown. "A haunting romance," claimed the cover — where I thought I'd written a feminist novel. I sent my children to buy up, one by one, the copies at the Vermont Book Store. The store later reported that the novel was a great success. The proprietor didn't know that one hundred naked-ladies-in-showers were stacked up at the Broken House in Cornwall.

The spring after the Scotland trip we went south to Williamsburg, Virginia. We'd study our country's history instead of our personal past; it seemed safer. I'd published a magazine article about a talented local puppeteer (it was his daughter who dove through our shop window). I was telling Spence about a phrase he had used — "coming down the strings" — to describe his rapport with his audience, when the phone rang. It was Catharine; her voice was thin and distraught, but grew stronger as she warmed to her tale. She'd invited a dozen friends and a few of *their* friends for an evening's gathering at the Broken House. Two hundred showed up as the word flashed through the high-school grapevine: "Parents away!"

"I hired a professional cleaner," she sobbed. "They were throwing up all over the place. But don't worry — the police got the stereo back."

"Remember, you're a writer," I told myself bravely on our return. After recovering from the shock of seeing my mother-in-law's horsehair sofa in three pieces, I sat the girl down to "record all" on tape. What would happen, I wondered as I replayed the tape, if a sensitive but sensible child like Catharine were born into a family of puppeteers, who turned night into day, sense into nonsense?

"Whatever became of that novel about me?" Catharine asked two years later, after *Down the Strings,* set in the Broken House in "Branbury," Vermont, had been rejected by one Virginia B. at Crown publishers and then stored away for eventual rewriting. (I'd gone back by then to my illegitimate grandmother.) Intimations of immortality shone in Catharine's eyes as she pointed out an ad in a writer's magazine: an editor from E.P. Dutton seeking young adult manuscripts.

Spence and I were in Florida this time when the call came. "The novel!" Catharine screamed over the wire: "She wants it!" "Who?" I yelled back. "That E.P. Dutton person," she hollered.

"You speak very well to teenagers," the letter confirmed, "and I think that the book will find a good audience." The letter was signed "Virginia B."

"Virginia B. probably had a stomach ache the first time she read it," said Spence. "I know I did."

We went to Yugoslavia on the advance. It was a "deal" we couldn't pass up: $755 included our round-trip flight and two weeks at a hotel outside the medieval walled city of Dubrovnik. Our balcony looked out on the Adriatic Sea. Although Spence wandered in and out and hung his socks to dry on its low iron railing, I suffered acute acrophobia whenever I looked down to the limestone piazza four stories below.

I was in bed, and Spence in the seventh-floor room of a Swedish ex-hockey star to continue a conversation we'd been having when the bar closed. They were sipping slivovitz and reliving the Olympics when the lights went out. There were no battery lights, no elevators; the place was a tomb as Spence crept down endless flights of stairs in search of the reception area that would lead him to our section of the hotel. He was exhausted and disori-

ented when at last an unlocked door gave way. He heard the
Adriatic beyond: in his relief he plunged forward and over the
railing.

Afterward we attributed his life to the plum brandy. He fell, it
appeared, like a baby — three flights down to the stone pavement,
where the night watchman found him.

"Vertay-bray. Pel-vees. Oomp!" said Dr. Brailo, who grunted
out his English in fractured nouns. My husband was a great white
mummy. Only his head and feet stuck out where he lay in the tiny
ward, sandwiched between two Yugoslavs, who stared out at us
from bandaged heads. Like the latter, the nurses spoke only Serbo-
Croatian. "Bedpan," murmured Spence, and they smiled and
melted away.

"Psst," Spence hissed at me after the doctor left. "See iv those
candles're still lit, would-ou?"

I said, "What candles?"

"Unnertha bed. They lit 'em to dry th' cast. Crawl unner an'
look, will-ou?"

"Morphine," said a nurse's aide, seeing my expression as I bent
to look, and pointing at Spence, rolled her eyes.

"Morphine," she repeated, and then hugged me, while I wept
on her blue shoulder.

I went back to my room and began a story called "The Leaper."
Writing it kept me sane for the next two weeks while I struggled
with Yugoslav bureaucracy. The question was how to bring my
stretchered husband home to the States. His back and pelvis were
broken and there was no sensation in one foot. We were down to
our last hundred dollars in travelers' checks. Seven years before,
we'd dropped our health insurance to pay college bills. Armed with
my Berlitz "Serbo-Croat for Travelers," I beat on the doors of bank
and airline, hospital and hotel management. The bank gave me
dinars for monies sent from home; the airline insisted I pay dollars.
As for the hotel, the "manager" smiled indulgently. The place was
run by a worker's coop — only Big Brother seemed to be in charge.

A medic must accompany us home, said the airline — for the
cost of a round-trip ticket. I found a radiologist who spoke English.
He'd be delighted, he said — for a small fee. He'd apply at once for
his visa. But he really should have an assistant, he said, with a

tender smile. (Three thousand dollars, I counted up, including two extra seats for the stretcher.) "A nine-hour flight, Meezes Wright? Vat cannot go wrong?"

"My bank account, that's what," said Spence, off the morphine now. "Tell him no. I'm not a cardiac case, for chrissake. All I need is a peanut butter jar!"

A week later the airline discovered we wouldn't need a medic at all if I would take full responsibility for my patient's welfare. "I will," I said, renewing the old vows made years before in the Middlebury Congregational Church. Nurses being in short supply, I'd become an old hand at feeding and watering Spencer and the two Yugoslavs. "Bye-bye," they waved each day as I left the room. "Laku noche," I cried, "u jutro!"

And so it went, until we took last-minute flight — literally, as the ambulances were all out — clutching x-rays and medical reports in Serbo-Croatian. Spence was upended like a piece of baggage and slid into the rear of the plane, where he held court to the passengers lining up for the toilets.

"My Aunt Hallie had a bad fall like that," one woman informed him.

"Is that right?" said Spence. "What happened to her?"

"Oh, she died," said the woman, and spun away into the lavatory.

It was a Marx Brothers landing. No one was informed in New York that a mummy case was aboard. A new crew came on, preparing to take off for Chicago. Then what looked like two angels came rushing up the aisle in ambulance armbands. One was Wedge Murdoch, the head broker in Spence's real estate firm. They zoomed his stretcher down a baggage elevator and into a Vermont ambulance. I imagined the headline: "100 Pounds of Heroin Smuggled Past U.S. Customs in Plaster Cast."

At home we found a hospital bed set up in the living room, the children there to greet us. "He looks like Uncle Chuck," Lesley whispered, "I can see the Wright bones in his face." We all blinked at one another, and then embraced. There in the iron bed, the invalid carried on his business via phone, and reigned like a king over what turned into a five-month cocktail party as friends, family, real estate and shop clients trooped into the Broken House, bearing books and bottles of wine. Spence's drink was strictly cranberry juice — for once we had the upper hand. He was photographed from every angle, a glass or an upraised bedpan in his hand, a wide grin on his face. "I never knew I had so many friends," he said.

"I did. And we're paying for it now." I stared woefully at the footprints on the living room floor. "You would pick the mud season to try to fly."

"Well, I found out one thing," he said. "I can't fly."

"Hooray! He admits it. Hear that, Clarissa?" I shouted. Upstairs in the closet there was a whooing sound of assent. I could always depend on Clarissa.

The friends were a help, though, hustling Spence in and out of the shop van, like a hutch or trestle table, as we delivered him here and there for tests. The $350 it cost us for two weeks in the Dubrovnik medical center grew into $6000 by the time we were done, with just one night in a U.S. hospital. But the high cost of falling was forgotten on the day he rose to take his first step. The physical therapist was on one side, and Catharine, just back from her own journey to the Middle East, on the other. Grandmother looked on with bright eyes. "Been down so long it looks like up to me," sang Catharine as her father struggled forward in his new brace, like an astronaut walking on the moon. He was twenty pounds lighter, but his hair still red withal.

His first outing on his own was to the tree farm. A year before the trip he'd started a new house, to be self-built in the heart of our fifteen acres. "No more lawn mowing," he'd declared, "the yard will be full of Christmas trees." It was early October, the children were all home for the weekend. The six of us drove up together, Spence erect behind the wheel. The peroneal nerve in his left leg was permanently damaged, causing a slight limp, but his back was straight and growing stronger every day.

"As long as we're all here," he said, eyeing his six-foot sons as they leaped out of the van (he was never one to pass up an opportunity), "we might as well get out some shovels. Got some footings to put in for the new house. Have to make up for lost time. I need you fellows on the beams, too."

"What's wrong with us women?" said Catharine. A Middlebury College junior, she was five foot-nine now, and running seven miles a day.

Her father squinted at her appraisingly. "Why, not a gaw-damn thing," he said, and sprang on ahead.

THE TREE FARM

Plus ça change, plus c'est la même chose.

Alphonse Karr, 19th century

Connecting Roots: Wright On

"HELLO!" SOMEWHERE IN THE HOUSE there was a banging on the door. I was upstairs writing a book about a couple who bought an old house in Vermont, and their subsequent adventures. In three months the manuscript was to be delivered to the publisher.

The banging came again. I bent to my work.

"Hello?" a man's voice shouted. "I want to buy a lamp!"

A lamp? I was winging my husband home from Yugoslavia. It was a long flight: a terror of turbulence while I clung to his stretcher . . .

"Can someone come out to the shop?"

The shop. I peered at my watch. It was eleven a.m. The shop was open. I'd forgotten to switch on the lights and activate the buzzer. There was no longer a saltbox labeled Pecunia. Now and then someone came into the shop and took something without paying. The world was encroaching on Vermont. Still, we clung to our faith system and let people wander unwatched — and most respected it. "Catharine!" I hollered. "Go out to the shop!"

"Wha—?" she called from her bed. "Oh. Shop?" Now a senior at Middlebury College, she'd been up all night writing her thesis, a novel. Between us, the new word processor I'd bought hummed around the clock. In the wee hours of the morning the printer roared and rumbled like the C&O freight trains that used to rock our cottage at Boys' Home, the haven for homeless lads where we worked during our first year of marriage.

I watched the fledgling novelist float out the kitchen door in her nightgown. The customer was a chemistry professor at the college. He smiled indulgently; he understood. But he wanted to buy a lamp.

The scene was repeated often in the following weeks. We were in transition. The shop and my new book were increasingly at odds: where the shop demanded people, my writing begged solitude. Although Spence managed to juggle trees and real estate, the three properties — lake, house, and tree farm — inevitably got out of hand. He'd dam up a leak in one house, to uncover a deluge in another. And the weeds grew with abandon. "Stop mowing your damn lawns!" he'd shout at the neighbors. Our front yard looked like the head of Rip Van Winkle, he said, between two shaved monks.

And there were the children, flying out of the nest and in again, piling up debris. Other couples talked about a generation gap between themselves and their offspring. To us, if there was ever a gap, it was filled at once. Donald, graduated from UVM and working with the retarded, lived with us for a time, then substituted books, boxes, and battered furnishings for his presence. Gary slapped a Do Not Throw Out sign on his beer can collection and his Apple Army paraphernalia, and went off to coach hockey at the University of Maine. Lesley went on staff at the Rochester Zen Center for a year, leaving behind her worldly goods, including her long-suffering James.

And there was Aunt Evelyn. Six months before Spence played Icarus from the hotel balcony, we had kidnapped her from a Nyack hospital and carried her back to Vermont. Like Spence, she took one step too many and pitched, at the age of eighty-six, down the dark stairs in her West Nyack house, breaking her arm. The next time, the doctor warned, it could be her head. "Who are you?" she demanded when he came in to examine her. He was no doctor, she insisted, she hadn't seen one of those in fifty years. "Why do you think I've lived so long?"

At the hospital she invited us into her "office." "That one types ninety words a minute," Evelyn said, pointing to the nurse. Two weeks later we packed up her house and bore her off to Vermont. By then she'd declared the hospital a "political prison." "They're all Democrats in here," she said. "They know I voted for Nixon." Well, this was the break-out, we said the morning we came for her. She was to keep mum until we crossed the state line. We suspect she knew where she was going, yet she played the game: "Hurry up!" she bawled, squinting out the rear window near Albany. "I think there's a cop on our tail!"

Since Mother Wright was still with us, we settled Evelyn into a retirement home run by friends in Middlebury. It had once been a college president's manse, and then a women's dormitory. (The elementary school Evelyn had attended as a child was across the street.) There she adopted the owner's cat, read the daily *Times* (after a cataracts operation), and opened up her "new office" to our visits. She was allowed her scotch but invited to give up cigarettes. Once a week Spence brought in Kenny Gorham, a classmate of Evelyn's, and the pair would hunch together over their grade school portrait. "Where's that one now?" Annie would ask, pointing out a befrocked and beribboned young girl. "Dead," Kenny would say. "And that fellow there?" she'd ask. "Dead," he'd say. "They're all dead." There would be a moment of silence. Then, "Time for a glass of scotch," she'd suggest. "Where in hell's that woman who runs this boarding house?"

The next fall we moved my sister Grace down to Middlebury. Retired from a lifetime of teaching, she suffered from Parkinson's Disease. She, too, settled into the retirement home, a bright spirit in a body that refused to cooperate, pitching her into corners she couldn't back out of. Twenty years apart and as different from each other as the Trylon obelisk from the ball-like Perisphere (in the 1939 New York World's Fair, where Grace used to give puppet shows), Evelyn and Grace managed to coexist, drawn together by the slow, unsteady pilgrimage to the Broken House for holidays and occasional outings.

Grace was bundled up on the porch one October afternoon, gold and russet leaves swirling about her head, when a car pulled in from downcountry. A young couple dashed into the shop. I was in my shorts, still in a state of collapse from the hustle jogs and flamingo flings of aerobic dance. Clarissa kept hiding my shorts on me, but I persevered.

"There's an old house down the street —," the man began.

"Still for sale? We thought you might know," she finished, a pretty black-haired woman with large, dark eyes.

"Oh, that was sold six months ago," I said. "But this one might be for sale." I glanced at their shiny red car, my eyes narrowed like Vivian LeDuc's three decades before.

"Can we look around?" she said eagerly.

"Why not? Oh, and the shop's for sale, too," I called after. They were already at the door. I heard their gasps as they took in the panorama of green fields speckled with cows, the mountains mauve with autumn.

"Who are they?" Grace whispered from the porch. The Parkinson's was wearing away her voice too, like a piano muted with dust.

"The new owners of Cornwall Crafts. Maybe," I qualified. It was important to sell the shop to just the right people.

The next day they were back. They'd been to my husband's real estate firm. Thompson-Rohrlich was their name. He was a psychologist, she a nurse, with a baby on the way. "I've never thought of running a shop," she said. "But I think I'd love it."

The closing was set for mid-June. "Ge-zum," said Spence, who felt swept along on a giant wave, "I guess I better get moving on that tree farm house."

"Uh huh. I mean, let's enjoy it before we have to move in with Grace and Auntie."

"Well —," he said.

"And that's the first step: water. I will *not* go back to the old days in the Broken House!"

He laughed and waved his hands.

Jim Ellefson arrived with a divining rod, a forked stick made of old applewood. Jim was a tall, lean, dark-bearded young man, a musician, poet, and blacksmith, with a heart as wide as his empty pockets and a sense of humor to match. Originally a friend of Lesley's, he came to us like a feral cat: we fed him pea soup, wine, and friendship — and he remained, an adopted son. He cut firewood and kept the van in running condition, the clocks wound and chiming in the shop. There were wildflowers on the table for me, and for the ladies in the retirement home. One Christmas he gave us the world. Moon, sun, and stars, hammered by Jim out of copper, swung about our shuddering wood stove.

The divining rod led inevitably to the western slope of the tree farm and the marshy area, a thousand feet from the house, that was a thin stream in spring and a dried mudbank in summer. To the north, and moving toward us like Birnum Wood to Dunsinane, was a series of beaver dams. The stick tugged in that direction. Jim and Catharine were swept off their feet, they said, behind the palpitating rod. "We got it!" Jim yelled up to Spence. "Prepare for the Deluge!"

"Bananas!" Spence yelled back, and hired his own necromancer. An elderly man recommended by the well driller, the dowser served as a kind of front man. "That ole black magic failed again," I imagined the driller telling his clients as he sank his rig ever deeper in the dry earth.

Although the dowser's wand yanked, like Jim's, in a northwesterly direction, a glance at Spence's face stopped him at a point one hundred twenty feet behind the new house. There he flung up a triumphant arm, like Spence's ancestor in early Cornwall making his pitch. The driller went to work. Three days later we received a call: "Down four hundred fifty feet — got just a trace. Whatdya think?"

"Keep going," said Spence, visions of evaporating dollar bills in his head.

By five hundred feet there was a full gallon per minute. I thought of my footed bathtub, a gift from Lesley and her husband, waiting outdoors for the move to "Spencer's Mountain." "I get to take the first bath," I said. "I mean, all two inches of it. You can hop in after me."

"Keep going," Spence told the well driller.

By six hundred feet he'd reached two gallons a minute. The bill was approaching five figures.

"Enough," said Spence, and the drilling rig lumbered away. I peered into a pit of mud and broken stone but could see no water at all. "How do you know it's there?" I asked.

"It's there," he said, his eyes narrowed with purpose.

"Well, in my opinion, you should have left it to the beavers."

One day in early spring we looked down to see a lake glimmering through the trees. "A mirage," said Spence.

"You think so?"

Down we tramped, Spence, Jim and I, our sneakers sinking into the spongy earth. The mirage grew into a full-size pond. And then another, where the beavers had crunched their way southward to construct a magnificent dam.

"It's magnificent all right," said Spence. "They've built it out of our trees."

"So what can you do? Beavers build. Writers write. Tree farmers farm trees."

"Not with those critters around they don't," said Spence.

"Hey, Spence — they got our firewood!" Jim cried.

The poplars Spence and Jim had hewn for firewood the fall before were gone. The beavers had dug a canal over to the pile and floated back the wood to incorporate it into their dam. Juniper and bull thistle were growing now where the wood pile had been.

"Someone's a dam fool," said Spence. "And I don't think it's the beavers."

To me the beavers were an asset, a glimmer of romance. "I mean, in case we ever resell," I told Spence that night. Think ahead. Way ahead, he always told his clients.

This time he shook his head vehemently. His hair was still red, I noticed, though faded from the carroty color of yesteryear. A few white wisps grew like dandelions in his mustache. "This is it," he said, "this is Home Sweet Home."

He'd built the new house out of old boards and beams, attaching it to the rear of the shop storage barn. The downstairs was L-shaped, with an airy writing room for me. The small-pane windows glanced out on a wonderland of trees and mountains — the Green Mountains to the east, the Adirondacks to the west. In spring the daisies and blue vetch wound about the branches of the pine trees. In summer and fall we'd find bird nests tucked inside, behind a camouflage of pine needles and Queen Anne's lace. As I looked I envisioned Christmas on the tree farm, the customers ascending as they did each season with kids, dogs, sleds, and grandmas; axes, hatchets, chain saws, plain saws — in pursuit of the perfect Christmas tree. "The Christmas Tree Follies," I called it in a piece I wrote for *Ford Times*. At the time I had mainly experienced the follies second hand while I ran the shop and took in the eight or nine dollars we charged for scotch pine or balsam. From now on I'd be caught up in the heart of the fevered dance. I shivered with anticipation. "I've got to keep up my aerobics!" I shouted at Clarissa as I dug through my chaotic closet. "Now deliver up my shorts, ghost!"

The new house would evolve about a great chimney to rise from basement to roof. For that purpose we hired a Scottish mason, a handsome, stocky man with a thick burr. His wife and I sang together in the church choir. He'd be here in July, he said. But when Spence called later that month: "Oh, aye. Well, August's the best time for chimneys."

"It's August, George," Spence reminded him the following month.

"Och, September, mon. Thot's the month to build chimneys. Much cooler then."

He arrived in mid October. For the edifice a friend had donated a heap of bricks pulled from an old driveway. They were worn and crumbly from years of heavy wheels. George gazed at them through lidded eyes.

"Shall I run some lines in?" said Spence.

"What for, mon?"

"So the chimney will be straight. I could run some lines from the basement to the ridge pole."

"The chimney will be straight," said George. And proceeded to build a thirty-four-foot chimney with a two-foot level. It rose straight as the Empire State Building and, to us, just as grand: the old beams and doors Spence had scavenged from friends and bygone hotels were the more crooked beside it. What Spence couldn't understand, though, was the nature of the "fawking bricks" of which George constantly complained.

"What's a 'fawking brick' anyway?" Spence asked one day, thinking it a variety he hadn't heard of.

"Here," said George. "Take a guid look." He flung out a handful of bricks: "This one's too long. This is too short. This, all chipped away. I'm supposed to piece the chimney together with these, mon? Dom fawking bricks, they are."

"Oh-h," said Spence, getting the point. "Well, come on, you can do it, George."

"You can do it," I said to Spence when he despaired of completing the house before mid-June. Henry Swider was unavailable now; his surveying and hunting trips out West kept him "geez, on the run, Spensah," as he said in one of his semi-annual visits to leave us a packet of antelope meat. But we had Lucien Charlebois, a neighbor and skilled carpenter, who came to help each Wednesday. A French-Canadian widower in his sixties, Lucien combined both Henry's honest industry and old Charlie's love of talk. I would drop in to the sound of belly laughter and the tinkle of ice as Spence and Lucien shared a cup or two of Old Cornwall. "Remember," I said one day in early May when I arrived on the scene to find the men heaving up the ancient beams but no sheetrock on the walls, no boards over the subfloors: "We have to be in here by June."

"My God," said Lucien, who was a worrier. "We'll never make it."

"Yes, you will," I said.

In some blind confidence that the house would rise out of the backs of those two middle-aged men, I dreamed and planned, pored through my mother-in-law's back issues of *House Beautiful.* Together Jim and I hacked a garden out of the rocky ledge, fertilized it with horse manure (a byproduct of Jim's blacksmithery), while the rabbits peered, bright-eyed, from the bushes. We called it Petticoat Strip, erected a sign and a pair of scarecrows: Victor and Anna Mae. We were connecting roots, after all. We put in rosemary and asparagus, bee-balm and broccoli. Jim brought in bees to pollinate the plants. On sunny days the bees sailed through the clover, wings glinting amber. On dull days we gave them a wide berth, at Jim's suggestion. "They're awful mad today," he'd say. We believed him the day he dashed up with thirty angry stings after trying to introduce a new queen into the hive.

"Maybe I should do that: get a new queen," Spence said when, armed with an article on "Beauteous Baths," I marched up to the new house to demand more space. The bathroom was six by eight feet. It would accommodate little more than the footed tub and the second-hand toilet he'd picked up (a new one would never hold up its lid to the old tub, he reasoned).

"So, who's worried?" I said. "No other woman would stand for this. We'll have to make out a peeing schedule."

"Don't worry about a thing, Nance," he said.

I tried not to. I directed a play for the Community Players, researched an article for a craft magazine. I nursed my husband through the aftermath of a hernia operation. He wasn't supposed to lift anything for six weeks, he complained. "So? We move June 16. That's six weeks and one day. You'll be ready," I told him. There was the job of inventorying the shop and ordering merchandise for the new owners. And there was Catharine's novel. We sat up nights in mid-April grinding out her finished copy on my printer. Every thirty pages or so the machine would grow hot and angry and spew out DDDD all over the page, and we'd all have to cool down and begin again.

For Spence there was the settling of his mother's estate. Ruth Wright had suffered a stroke that fall, and passed away quietly at the age of eighty-six. We had a lot of singing at her funeral, as she'd requested. And Spence and his brothers told old stories: about dragging in a forest tree, for instance, each midnight Christmas Eve, and her struggle to decorate it at two in the morning. "She loved ceremony," Spence observed, "but she didn't get much help from the Wright men. Yet she learned to hold her own, as all of you well know. She was a true matriarch." "Amen," I murmured in the front pew.

"All the ceremonies of our lives," I said to Spence three weeks before the move. "Weddings. Holidays. Funerals. Packing up, and unpacking. Planting and chopping down. Sometimes I wonder how we go on."

"That's it," he said. "We just go on. We keep planting. Or fall through the hole."

"What hole? In the universe, you mean?"

"In the new house," he said. "Where the cellar steps are supposed to be. Jim fell through today."

"No! Didn't you put up a sign?"

"I put cardboard over the opening. To keep out the cold."

"Nice going," I said, "a neat camouflage." I got the story from

Jim. He'd been searching for a wrench on the tool shelf by the missing stairway. "Where are you, Jim?" Spence hollered, needing a hand with a hunk of lumber.

"Down here," Jim gasped, "in the cellar." Barely recovered from the thirty bee stings, he saw purple bruises swelling up on his limbs.

"Well, come on up here! I can't lift this two-by-four alone, you know."

The next one to fall through was Rick, a carpenter-musician known as Chicken Wing because of his vigor with the bass fiddle in Jim's band. He was employed in our time of crisis to lay the living room floor. His famous wing failed him when he backed onto the cardboard, and still clutching a can of nails, catapulted down into the rocky hole.

"Damn it!" said Spence. "You guys are busting up all my cardboard!"

The third victim was Terry, a gangly six-foot-two-inch classmate of Catharine's, a classics major, who came to find solace with us after the defection of his girl friend. We settled him in a bed surrounded by tools and paint cans, and offered him food and water in the Broken House in return for his labor. While vacuuming up the sawdust, he leaned forward to pick up a fallen brush and dove head first through the hole. He thought he was in heaven as stars exploded about his head.

"Did you drop something?" Lucien called out. And peering down, bellowed: "Hey, Spence! You got another one in the trap!"

A week before the exodus we cleaned out the hut and other black holes of the Broken House, and held a garage sale. We sold everything from BB guns to chamber pots (you might need those, Spence warned, and absconded with one). The hut bureau went for $15.50. (The fifty cents was for the family of mice curled up in the drawers. I saw Virginia Graham's hair ribbon nod in the shadows.) Someone offered ninety-five cents for the beer can collection, but we held off loyally. "At least save my letters from the hut," Gary had appealed over the phone. He was about to take on a head coaching job at American International College in Massachusetts, and had to start work at once. "I knew he'd get out of the move," said Catharine. Her disappointment was doubled to find that the letters were not love notes, but athletic Ps. "I give up on him," she said, turning away, as he had once abandoned Olympian hopes for her when she refused to circle the pond for the three-hundredth time.

We packed by day, and painted and sanded the new house by night. The more belongings we packed, the more sprang out of the woodwork. My painted walls, so pristine white at night, appeared streaked and full of gaps in the morning light. "You pack; Terry and I paint," Spence decreed.

Terry painted more than the walls. We received a call one wee hour from a local bartender to come and get the lad, who was drowning his girlfriend's memory in bloody marys. Supported into the new house between Spence and Catharine, he insisted he would paint, not go to bed: "Tha' wall ove' there," he said, "whatoo want me do wi'it?"

"Prime it," said Spence.

"Pr-rime it," said Terry, fitting his tongue carefully around the words. "Prr-rime it. Lemme avea brush."

"Tomorrow," said Spence wisely.

"T'morrow an' t'morrow," said Terry

"And tomorrow," Catharine concluded. And everyone, wisely, went to bed.

The next morning Terry stumbled on the steps and sprained his ankle under the collected works of Victor Hugo. In the afternoon someone removed a supporting bookcase, and the trap door fell shut on his head. An hour later he was all but castrated, he screamed, as Catharine, on the back end of a chest of drawers, rammed him into a door that suddenly swung to. He retired to his paint can.

As we drew into the final days the packing became more frenetic. Bits of several rooms were thrown at random into the same unlabeled box. The freezer, en route from the pantry, spewed out a jetstream of water that flooded the kitchen. A toilet that had held out for years suddenly let go. The tractor lost its brakes as it reeled recklessly down Route 30 with the home-made beds, a broken spinning wheel, a World War I shell full of old gunpowder, and two hundred *Better Homes & Gardens* that had somehow multiplied over the decades in the heat of the shop attic.

Our offspring clung, giggling, to the rear. They might have been off on a childhood expedition to lug marble or knock down an old barn.

Two and a half days before Move Day, company arrived. A poet, golfer, and colleague from our school days who was now teaching in a Canadian university, Claude Liman pedaled into our yard with his wife Ellen. Exhausted and in pain from the long bicycle ride, Ellen burst into tears on arrival. They were here to spend a few days, said Claude, confused at seeing the dismantled house. He'd written in a Christmas note, he reminded us, that they might come in June.

We settled them into the small lake camp and lent them a car. In return, they offered us a hand in the moving. Ellen, Catharine, and Jim moved out the final pieces while I scrubbed in their wake. During most of the madness Claude sat hunched before the TV, mesmerized by the Golf Nationals, while Spence made five gallons of wine and cut up onions for a batch of pea soup. "It'll be a while before the stove is hooked up," he warned.

On M-Day itself one of our veteran salesmen, a gregarious Irishman who'd been wounded in World War II, limped in to sell his new line of baskets, clocks, and pots. He jogged along beside me as I bore out boxes to the van. "I promised the new owners to go light on the buying," I told him, as I heaved a clamor of pots into the rear of the vehicle.

"They'll buy up these clocks like hot cakes," he said. "Gee whiz, get rid of what you've got in there on the wall. Schoolhouse clocks are out, I'm telling you. Banjos are in." He trotted back to the house with me.

"I've already got a couple of those," I said. "You sold them to me three years ago."

"Oh, really?" he said. "Well, keep plugging them, then."

He was backing out with his clocks and baskets, still hollering his sales pitch out the car window, when the Buttolph girls pulled in. Dynamic maiden ladies in their sixties who once ran an informal "Kid's Camp" that included our two youngest, they were down to visit their brother Tom. Mabel rushed up to throw her arms around us. "I can see it's a bad time," she gushed. "But I haven't seen you all in a dog's age. With old friends you never know when it'll be too late."

"It might be too late," I said, standing before her like my pale closet-ghost. "But have a glass of something with us anyway." The last gallon of Old Cornwall, Spence had prudently advised, was to go in the last load.

A daughter of old Lute, Mabel joined us. Into her second glass, she recalled that her sister, Grace, was waiting in the car. "I make it a point never to visit folks when they're moving!" Grace Buttolph shouted as we advanced on her.

"Well you may never see them again!" Mabel hollered back, her face pink and trembly.

"Where are you moving to?" asked Grace. "Alaska?"

"Up the road," I said. "Half a mile."

"Well, then," said pragmatic Grace. "Get in the car, Mabel. A move is a move, and these folks don't need us today." She revved up the engine as Mabel waved frantically after us.

Overcome by it all, Catharine wept. Unable to face a last night in the Broken House, she threw down her sleeping bag among the trees outside the new house.

Spence, the cat, and I slept alone in the old house that last night, on a disembodied mattress. Sometime in the night, I sat up in bed, hearing a noise.

"Whazzit?" said Spence.

"Sh-h. A sound. A kind of squealing."

"A squirrel."

"Not a squirrel. A voice. Like a sighing."

"Wind."

"Clarissa," I said. "She's weeping. She doesn't want us to leave. Hear? Oh, definitely, it's Clarissa."

"Clarissa? Tha' girlfriend of Donald's?"

"That's Terrell. I mean Clarissa, my ghost. I hope she'll like the new people. They have a baby boy now, you know."

"She'll like 'em. Now go azleep."

"Clarissa," I whispered. "A new baby. Think of that." And the sound ceased.

Early the next morning we took a last shower in the old stall we'd appropriated from school, then loaded in mattresses, boxes full of shredded wheat and toothbrushes, the cat's dish, the gallon of Old Cornwall, my typewriter (the word processor would wait until the sawdust settled), and rattled off in the van to the tree farm.

"What about water? We'll have it in a couple of days?"

"Water?" said Spence, preoccupied with his thoughts.

"Water. H_2O. To bathe in, flush with, water the plants. I mean, you've told the plumber we're moving in?"

"Oh, sure. But we have to dig first. Couple of trenches. The septic system, all that. I'll call Ralph this morning to come and backhoe."

"You haven't called him yet?"

"We've been moving. What time have I had?"

"Then what? After the trenches?"

"Then we get the plumber. To lay the pipes. Connect up."

"Then?"

"We'll have water going out."

"And coming in?"

"That, too. Eventually."

"When? When is eventually?" We were rounding the bend of Cider Mill Road. The cat sat between us, howling. Ahead was our driveway. The new house stood solid and dry on the crest of the green hill.

"Two, three weeks maybe. But don't worry. It's all set up."

So it was. There were the sawhorses joined by the wide plank. The five gallon jug. The dipper pan. The chamber pot he'd salvaged from the garage sale.

"We're lucky to have it so private up here," he said. "No one can see."

"Mmm."

"Look by the door," he said. "Surprise."

Wild roses, I saw. White, with yellow centers. Freshly transplanted from the Broken House by Jim and Doc Collier. They were starting to droop, though, from the shock of transplanting. I watered them with my tears.

"They'll grow," said Spence, putting his arms around me.

"It's not that," I said. "It's not the water either. It's — it's all those years, I guess. And now the kids grown up. Even Catharine out of school."

"I know," he said.

"But they'll be back. For holidays and all. And it'll be kind of fun. Just you and I and the trees. Don't you think?"

"Yup," he said, squeezing my arm. And he hopped up the steps.

Inside, the cat had found the cardboard-covered hole to the basement. Unlike the other victims, she'd landed on her feet. Her green eyes gazed up at us, astonished.

"At least," I said, "we won't have to get up and let her out all the time."

"I told you."

"Told me what?"

"That you'd have all the room you need. All the privacy. Even the cat won't bother you."

"Shh. Listen —"

"The cat. Trying to get out of the basement."

"Not the cat. Hear?"

Outside, a car was screeching to a halt. A moment later Donald burst in the house with his girlfriend. He'd given up his Burlington apartment, he said, "It'll be cheaper this summer to commute from here."

"Terry wants to stay another week. You don't mind, do you? He'll work," said Catharine, running in behind him.

Spence's eyes lit up at the word 'work.' "You're all aware," I said, "that we have no water."

"No problem," said Donald, "I like camping out in the trees."

The cat arrived at the front door, howling to be let in. Spence placated her with a handful of Tender Vittles. "What's that you were telling me?" I asked him. "About having all the room I'd need? All the you-know-what?"

"Exactly," he said. "All for you. And Lucien just built you some shelves. Go in and take a look."

I peered through the doorway of my new writing room. Sure enough, there were three tiers of shelves lining the white walls — enough space for at least four hundred books. Overhead, the beams from Victor Wright's barn stretched across the room. Old barnboard framed the windows that glanced out on the trees, and beyond, at the Green Mountains.

"Not bad," I said, blinking at the view. "Not bad at all."

Out in the kitchen the cat meowed again, and Catharine shushed it. I cleared away a space and set up my typewriter on a packing box.